SYSTEMS OF PROFIT MEASUREMENT

SYSTEMS OF PROFIT MEASUREMENT

John Baillie, MA, CA
Johnstone Smith Professor of Accountancy
University of Glasgow

Partner of Thomson McLintock/KMG
Chartered Accountants

Published for
THE INSTITUTE OF CHARTERED
ACCOUNTANTS OF SCOTLAND
by
GEE & CO (PUBLISHERS) LIMITED

A Gee text first published in 1985 by
Van Nostrand Reinhold (International) Co. Ltd
11 New Fetter Lane, London EC4P 4EE

Reprinted 1987, 1989

Photoset in 9 on 11 point Times by
Kelly Typesetting Ltd, Bradford-on-Avon, Wiltshire
Printed in Hong Kong

Library of Congress Cataloging in Publication Data

Baillie, John.
Systems of profit measurement.
"Published for the Research Advisory Committee of the Institute of Chartered Accountants of Scotland"—
1. Income accounting. 2. Corporations—Accounting.
I. Title.
HF5681.I48B34 1985 657'.48 84-21578
ISBN 0-85258-234-X

Foreword

This series of monographs has been initiated by the Research Advisory Committee of The Institute of Chartered Accountants of Scotland. It is addressed to all groups with an interest in accounting information.

At a time of change and of increasing interest in accounting information the Committee believes that these monographs will meet a need for explanation of some of the more difficult concepts underlying the preparation of corporate accounting reports which will be understandable to readers who are not familiar with the extensive academic theoretical literature on the subject. Although primarily intended for accountants, bankers, civil servants, directors and managers, and investors and their advisers, they have also been found useful for students.

The Committee commends the monographs for study and discussion in the interests of better understanding; the opinions expressed by the authors are, of course, their own.

The subject with which this monograph deals is one of concern to all of these groups, many of whose members find it a puzzling situation that there is not one single unique method of measuring profit and that each alternative method has a logical and theoretically sound basis. The monograph is devoted to explaining briefly "how" and "why".

The Institute of
Chartered Accountants
of Scotland

David Flint
Convener, Research Advisory Committee

Contents

Preface

The contemporary debate about systems of profit measurement has intensified in the UK in the last ten years or so and has centred on the argument about accounting for changing price levels and/or inflation.

Like beauty, the measurement of profit tends to be in the eye of the beholder. The preferences for this concept of income measurement, or that variation, are wide and varied and strongly held. Yet on these varying interpretations and measurements of the *same* economic circumstances can depend profound and far-reaching investment decisions for an enterprise, decisions which, collectively, make up a substantial part of the economic activity of the nation and which, therefore, affect the market supply of and demand for those three economic factors of production – materials, labour and capital.

Alongside this continuing debate about preferred income models is the conflict between the user who, understandably, wants as much information as is relevant, presented simply, and the specialist preparer, who sees only too clearly the dangers inherent in satisfying the user demand for simplicity at the expense of a good understanding of the complex economic issues which can be involved. These dangers include that of the user reaching the wrong decision based on, and as a consequence of, information so spuriously simple as to be facile.

It is against this background that I have written this monograph at the invitation of the Research Advisory Committee of The Institute of Chartered Accountants of Scotland. It is an exposition of the six main models of income measurement, an exposition which is aided (I hope) by a simplified example which interprets the same basic data according to the income concept under discussion. I have tried to avoid as much technical language as I can, although this has put even greater pressure on space already severely limited for a subject so vast in its scope; these limitations have precluded any real departure from each main theme to explain the significant variations usually encountered. In short I have tried to keep the terminology straightforward while restricting discussion to the principal approach of each of the six models. I hope the reader will forgive any failure of the former and undue success of the latter!

The monograph, which is in nine chapters, is aimed primarily at those preparers and users of, and those interested in, financial information who seek a greater understanding of the issues involved in the measurement of profit. After two opening chapters which identify and discuss these issues the text addresses, in succeeding chapters, each of the six main income models in turn and after explaining their main features, using the simplified example, identifies the perceived strengths and weaknesses; these strengths and weaknesses are presented in a different typeface to alert the reader seeking only an overview of the distinguishing features of each model that this part of the discussion may be regarded as optional reading. The last chapter summarises the discussions and considers alternative measures of economic progress towards the fragile and elusive concept of income.

I am deeply indebted to the members of the Research Advisory Committee, and particularly to its Convener, Professor David Flint, of the University of Glasgow, for the wise and helpful comments and suggestions received as well as for the patience shown and the encouragement given. This help was invaluable.

Responsibility for opinions expressed in this monograph, and for any shortcomings, remain, of course, with me.

John Baillie

Prologue – Profit Measurement: What's the Problem?

The problem illustrated

Consider this: Mr X decides to open a dairy. He buys property with some help from his local bank. He also buys two vans. He collects the processed and bottled milk every day from his supplier and pays for it on collection; thus there are no trade creditors. He either delivers this milk to customers or sells it in the dairy. Those customers to whom he delivers pay weekly. There is no inventory (that is, stock of trading goods comprising raw materials, components, work in progress, finished goods or goods for resale); debtors are minimal and, for our purposes, can be ignored. Tax can also be ignored.

After close of trading at the end of the third year Mr X retires. He scraps the vans, sells the property and pays off the bank loan.

Price movements and transactions

		Beginning of Year 1	End of year 1	2	3
Property – cost		£8,000			
of which –					
funded by X	£6,000				
loaned by bank at 10% pa	2,000				
– estimated replacement cost			£8,900	£9,900	
– estimated realisable value			8,800	9,700	
– actual sale proceeds					£11,500
(Property is not depreciated – contrary to the provisions of SSAP 12)					
Vans (2) – cost (each)		3,900			
all funded by X					
– cost to replace new, each			4,500	5,400	6,000
– estimated useful life – 3 years					
– estimated realisable value, each			2,900	1,500	—
– actual proceeds (scrapped)					—
General inflation measured by government index of general purchasing power		100	110	121	132
Operating data					
Sales			£12,000	£19,000	£23,000
Purchases of milk and other expenses (including interest) paid – original cost			9,000	14,000	17,000

Balance sheet
The opening balance sheet, at the beginning of year 1, is therefore:

Property	£8,000
Vans (2 × £3,900)	7,800
	15,800
representing –	
Capital contributed by X	13,800
Bank loan	2,000
	15,800

(The initial amount of cash needed to purchase milk and pay expenses has been ignored for simplicity)

Profit

According to different theories of profit measurement the progress and success of the enterprise can be variously represented:

Income concept	Profit in year 1	2	3	Holding gains (or windfalls)	Total
Historical cost	£400	£2,400	£3,400	£3,500	£9,700
General purchasing power applied to historical cost	340	1,754	2,023	940	5,057
Replacement cost	—	1,400	2,000	6,300	9,700
Current cash equivalent (before capital maintenance adjustment)	1,800	3,100	4,800	—	9,700
Economic value (ex post)	1,765	1,942	2,137	3,856	9,700
Value to the firm	13	1,400	2,000	6,287	9,700

There are significant interperiod variations in the profit reported but, aside from the general purchasing power method, these are equalised by holding gains (or a windfall gain in the case of economic income) to give the same aggregate money increment to Mr X over the three-year period; namely £9,700. Put another way, Mr X has realised an excess of £9,700 in cash after maintaining his opening money capital:

Opening capital in year 1	£13,800
Closing capital distributed to Mr X at the end of year 3	23,500
Excess	£9,700
made up of –	
Sales	£54,000
Purchases of milk and other expenses	(40,000)
	14,000
Net cost of property and vans (£15,800 – £11,500)	(4,300)
	£9,700

1 Profit and Periodic Measurement

The essence of accounting

An economic entity, like our dairy, holds a fluctuating stock of scarce resources in which it deals over a period. This activity causes flows in and out of the stock and, conversely, the flow explains the changes to the stock; the measurement of one is interdependent on the other. Periodic financial statements which are customarily in use can be divided into two types. The first type is the statement of the stock of resources and the claims on this – that is, the balance sheet. The second type is the flow statement; and there are many examples of this, such as the statement of income (or gains), which explains the net change to the stock of resources, and the cash flow statement, which shows why the amount of this particular stock (cash) has changed. The essence of accounting is the measurement and reporting of the stocks and flows, and much accounting debate and controversy comes down to this.

Profit and the relevance of its measurement

The focus of this text is the measurement of income or profit. While it may seem obvious that a primary objective of commercial enterprises organised for profit is, in fact, profit, it will be worthwhile, before proceeding, to confirm that this is so and that the measurement of it is therefore considered relevant.

For example, in a comparative study of four major works on income measurement, published in 1976 by the American Accounting Association, there was unanimity about the motive of the firm being profit maximisation.[1] In 1975 *The Corporate Report* indicated that some 58% of chairmen in the larger UK listed companies linked primary objectives to profits (including 10% who related profit directly and only to shareholders).[2] This may appear to be a surprisingly low figure. However, almost all those in the remaining 42% indicated or implied that profit was one of several objectives of equal status with, for example, customer service, employee welfare and serving the environment and society at large. Again, in discussing the reasons for income measurement, Lee states:

> Income is an important element of the capitalist, free-enterprise economy. It symbolizes wealth accumulation, and characterizes success in such a system: the bigger the income, the larger the assumed success. (Many individuals would, of course, disagree, on social and political grounds, with this crude comparison.) There does indeed exist a significant goal in the free-enterprise economic model – that of income maximization.[3]

Users

It seems clear that, if the singular or shared primary objective of an entity is profit, a statement which reports on the measurement of profit is relevant. This should provide a means of evaluating achievement of the objective, past performance and decisions and, thereby, a basis for predicting the future and making decisions accordingly. In preparing such statements, however, we need to have in mind the users and their needs. Both *The Corporate Report*[4] and the Government-sponsored Sandilands Report,[5] for example, identified comprehensive lists of potential users of general-purpose reports; these comprised a wide range covering equity investors, loan creditors, employees, management, analysts and advisers, customers, suppliers, competitors, government, consumers, environmental protectionists and pressure groups. There is also the qualitative status of the user to be considered, ranging from the layman to the expert. This is an issue addressed by Keane in his discussions of the efficient market hypothesis.[6]

Interestingly, two of the four main works considered by Anderson in his comparative study[7] believed that, particularly, management needs for income-based information had some priority (although this was related to all such information, not simply to general-purpose reports). But while these user requirements are wide and varied, Lee provides a useful summary:

> [they] all have one thing in common – they need income data with which to make and monitor decisions. In other words, reported income measurements are generally conceived as being useful for predicting and comparing with future data.[8]

Periodic measurement and incomplete transactions

A clear distinction was drawn earlier between the stock of scarce resources on the one hand and the flows in and out of this stock on the other. In the context of an entity's entire lifespan the distinction may be of little relevance. An entity starts with a stock of resources and, however much later, ends with a stock which is then distributed. Given that most entities have an indeterminate life, this latter event cannot usually be anticipated.

Often this stock is in the form of cash, but it need not be. When an entity starts, non-cash resources may be contributed. Again when an entity ends, part or all of the resources distributed may be in a non-cash form. Examples of such resources are property, and plant and equipment. Usually there are few problems in measuring the value of such resources at these times because there is an implied or actual transaction involving a willing supplier and a willing recipient. All stock, however, is expressed in cash or cash equivalent terms representing the store of value – that is, the extent of command over economic resources. Given the relative ease of determining the value of non-cash resources at the beginning and end of an entity, this text assumes for simplicity of explanation that all resources at the beginning and end of an entity are in cash.

The fundamentally important focus, at both dates, is the stock of resources. At the latter date it may also be of interest to know how the entity came to have the amount of the stock then held. And it may also be of interest to refine this further by adjusting for money contributed by, or returned to, the owners of the entity to determine how much of any change to the stock was made up by gains (or losses).

This leads to the question "what are gains?" and the related one, "what is income?". And they are given further importance if interim, or periodic, measurements of progress are needed. The distinction between stocks and flows then becomes highly relevant. There seems little doubt that such periodic measurements are needed, given the profit motive on the one hand and the potentially long life of the entity on the other. Hendriksen puts it like this:

> The overall measurement of income for the entire life of the enterprise does not provide the information when it is most useful, nor does it describe the causes of success or failure. Success may be the result of good fortune or efficient management. The sources or causes of income are thus important in a proper evaluation of the progress of the firm.[9]

The fundamental additional problem which periodic measurement creates is that of incomplete transactions or exchanges. Anderson quotes Sterling on the matter:

> Indeed the underlying problem can be stated as a desire for income measurement when the exchange is incomplete.[10]

The problem which arises relates to the periodic measurement of assets in non-cash form. As we shall see shortly there are several main concepts of asset measurement. Generally, however, the closer to realisation into cash that an asset is the fewer are the uncertainties and problems associated with its evaluation. It will be useful at this stage to mention in passing the classification of assets into monetary and non-monetary. Monetary assets are fixed in terms of the number of monetary units in which they are expressed and are relatively straightforward to value – for example, cash and debtors. Non-monetary assets are those which are not fixed in these terms – for example, equipment and inventories. There can be significant evaluation problems with non-monetary assets relating to price changes.

The purpose of this monograph

The wide and intensive interest in the measurement of periodic income on the one hand and the quite disparate interperiod valuations which can arise from the use of different income models on the other suggest that there is merit in identifying and in understanding the principal sources of such disparity. This text seeks to do just that – namely, to identify the principal features of each of the six main models of income measurement and to explain these features in a straightforward manner unencumbered by unnecessary technical language.

It is hoped, therefore, that this monograph will promote an understanding of the issues and problems of income measurement sufficient to enable the reader to select the model most appropriate to his needs at any time.

Approach taken

Chapters 3 to 8 are devoted to a discussion of each of the six main models of income measurement which were identified in the opening illustrative example:

Chapter 3 – the historical cost model
Chapter 4 – the general purchasing power model
Chapter 5 – the replacement cost model
Chapter 6 – the current cash equivalent model
Chapter 7 – the economic income model
Chapter 8 – the mixed value to the firm model

Each is compared and contrasted, in turn, against a "grid" of those factors which are considered key variables in the measurement of income. These key variables are:

– the measurement property of the monetary unit
– the basis of the asset valuation
– the concept of capital to be maintained
– the classification of holding gains (or windfalls)

Limitations on space mean that the discussion necessarily concentrates on the main features of each model to the exclusion of many of the detailed variations possible. It is believed, however, that all the significant contentious issues are thereby thrown into relief. Explanation of each model is assisted by a simple worked example based on the information given earlier.

At the end of each chapter the "case for" and the "case against" the income model is presented, based on an examination of informed opinion from the literature and the documentary evidence in the references. The author also offers his own comments on each income model. This discussion of the "case for" and the "case against" may be regarded as optional reading by the reader who seeks only an overview of the distinguishing features of each model.

Throughout the text the terms "income" and "profit" are used interchangeably. The reader, however, may detect greater use of the former term, since it is the more conventional.

Before embarking on a discussion of each income model it will be useful to consider the nature of income and those various factors on which its measurement depends, particularly the key variable factors identified above. This is done at Chapter 2, which also contains a résumé of those characteristics which contribute to the achievement of usefulness – that quality generally considered to be central to the measurement and disclosure of financial and accounting information.

References and notes

1. J. A. Anderson, "A Comparative Analysis of Selected Income Measurement Theories in Financial Accounting". Studies in Accounting Research Number 12, by the American Accounting Association, 1976, page 23.
   The major works compared were:
   Y. Ijiri, *The Foundations of Accounting Measurement*, Prentice-Hall, 1976.
   E. O. Edwards and P. W. Bell, *The Theory and Measurement of Business Income*, University of California Press, 1961.
   R. R. Sterling, *The Theory and Measurement of Enterprise Income*, The University of Kansas Press, 1970.
   D. Solomon's revision of earlier work by S. Alexander. "Income Measurement in a Dynamic Economy" in Baxter and Davidson, *Studies in Accounting Theory*, Richard D. Irwin, 1962.
2. The Corporate Report, A discussion paper. The Accounting Standards Steering Committee, 1975. Paragraph 4.27 and Appendix 4. Of a survey of the 300 largest listed companies in the UK 58% of the 166 chairmen replying saw primary corporate objectives linked to profits.
3. T. A. Lee, *Income and Value Measurement, Theory and Practice* (2nd edition), Van Nostrand Reinhold (UK) Limited, 1980, page 20.
4. The Corporate Report, paragraph 1.9.

5. F. E. P. Sandilands, "Inflation Accounting". Report of the Inflation Accounting Committee, HMSO, 1975, page 43.
6. S. M. Keane, *The Efficient Market Hypothesis and the Implications for Financial Reporting*. A monograph of The Institute of Chartered Accountants of Scotland, 1980; out of print.
7. J. A. Anderson, "A Comparative Analysis of Selected Income Measurement Theories in Financial Accounting", page 35.
8. T. A. Lee, *Income and Value Measurement*, page 23.
9. E. S. Hendriksen, *Accounting Theory* (3rd edition), Richard D. Irwin Inc, 1982, page 161.
10. J. A. Anderson, "A Comparative Analysis of Selected Income Measurement Theories in Financial Accounting", page 17.

2 What Determines Profit Measurement?

What is profit?

There have been many attempts at defining income or profit, and the definitions vary considerably with the concept advocated. Many writers of accounting literature start by looking to the economist's view of income, and here Fisher[1] is usually quoted as the original authority on personal income. He viewed income as a flow of goods and services enjoyed by consumption through time, and capital as a stock of wealth represented by the future goods and services still to be enjoyed by consumption. There was, therefore, a clear distinction drawn between capital and income. Earlier Adam Smith had defined personal income as the amount that could be consumed without using up capital. Hicks then refined this:

> The purpose of income calculations in practical affairs is to give people an indication of the amount they can consume without impoverishing themselves. Following out this idea it would seem that we ought to define a man's income as the maximum value which he can consume during a week, and still expect to be as well off at the end of the week as he was at the beginning.[2]

"Welloffness" was measured by the discounted present value of future anticipated receipts. Hendriksen, in referring to the perception of personal enjoyment by Fisher, has pointed out that a business enterprise, in contrast, does not exist for the purpose of enjoyment. Thus, translating the concept to a business environment, he described income as the flow of wealth or services in excess of that necessary to maintain a constant capital.[3] "Economic income", as this concept is often termed, will be discussed more fully in the context of business enterprises (see Chapter 7).

Again, as a further example, the Sandilands Committee defined the profit of a company in the following terms:

> A company's profit for the year is the maximum value which the company can

> distribute during the year, and still expect to be as well off at the end of the year as it was at the beginning.[4]

There appears then to be general acceptance that income cannot be said to have been earned until capital has been maintained. Put another way, income represents the increase in net wealth after providing for capital maintenance. Such an increase in net wealth assumes, of course, that further capital contributions by proprietors and distributions to them are first taken account of before any change in net wealth is determined. In this text this assumption is implicit in references to changes to net wealth and capital.

What capital?

The foregoing discussion may have highlighted one of the fundamental questions of income measurement: if "welloffness", or opening capital, has to be maintained before income can be said to have been earned, to what "capital" does this refer? Accounting literature and theory abound with contenders and there are variations on each theme. The principal concepts of capital maintenance, however, are original money capital, replacement capital (usually representing operating capacity), current cash equivalent capital (based on realisable values), the present value of future benefits (the economic income concept) and purchasing power capital (which takes account of the problem of the changing general price level and the effect this has on the stability of the monetary unit used to measure and express capital). There is, in addition, the value of assets to the firm concept of capital which is based upon a mixture of the other concepts. An example of this is known in the UK as current cost accounting and has received much attention relatively recently in being recommended by the Sandilands Committee[5] and in being adopted by Exposure Draft 35 and its predecessor SSAP 16.[6] Other countries have also adopted variations of it.[7] Each of the principal concepts mentioned above is discussed more fully in succeeding chapters.

Assets and their measurement

To check whether capital has been maintained, on whatever concept, it is necessary to value it. This requires evaluation of the stock of resources which repesents it and there are various valuation bases available. But, before discussing these bases, it will be helpful to first consider what is meant by "resource": that is, in order to qualify for evaluation what qualities should a resource possess?

Chambers defines as asset as "any severable means in possession of an entity".[8] The emphasis on severability is subsequently used by Chambers to justify his view of the basis of asset evaluation (see discussion on current cash equivalent income model at Chapter 6). McDonald refers to assets as "stocks of concern because they represent scarce exchangeable resources". For example, a stock of concern is debtors because it represents an exchangeable resource.[9] Note again the emphasis on exchangeability. Earlier, Canning had defined an asset as:

> . . . any service in money or any future service convertible into money (except those services arising from contracts the two sides of which are proportionately unperformed) the beneficial interest in which is legally or equitably secured to some person or set of persons to whom it runs.[10]

Here a particular emphasis is on the exclusivity of entitlement. Hendriksen attempted to summarise the qualities as follows:

(1) There must be some specific right to the future positive benefit or service potentials. Expired rights are not assets nor are rights with negative potential.
(2) The right must accrue to a specific entity to the exclusion of others (although sharing with other specific entities still qualifies).
(3) The right must be able to be utilised so that it or other assets are severable.
(4) The claim to the right must be legally enforceable (but this does not necessarily mean a formal legal title or contract).[11]

Identification of the existence of assets is only one part of the problem; recognition is another. A particularly difficult issue is whether to recognise intangible assets such as goodwill. Goodwill, meaning here the expectation of future income as a consequence of the many and diverse efforts of the entity to develop a reputation for good and reliable products and/or services, is not recognised by most income models. Instead recognition is deferred until, if ever, a transaction occurs which focuses attention on goodwill; for example, the purchase of the entity by another. At that point the price paid includes the purchaser's estimate of the future anticipated income as well as a view of the value, to it, of each of the entity's other assets. Until this point, however, the accounting recognition of this internally generated goodwill is usually restricted by convention.

Initially assets are expressed by description and, if they are also tangible, by quantities. They cannot be aggregated meaningfully without being reduced to a common mode of expression. That common mode is the monetary unit and the application of this unit to the disparate descriptions and quantities is the valuation process. As indicated earlier, much accounting debate is about the valuation process. As McDonald puts it, "Accounting reports are aggregations of unlike quantities weighted by prices" and, as he points out, the debate about which particular basis of valuation to adopt is a debate about the weights (prices) which are most appropriate.[12] Ijiri refers to the monetary unit as the "basic class" in which all other resources are conventionally measured; that is, money.[13]

There are three fundamental valuation bases available – past values, current values and future values. Past values are those typically adopted in historical cost accounting where only the original acquisition costs are considered relevant.

Current values, in contrast, focus on the market values obtaining at the reporting date. There are two approaches to current value – entry-to-the-market prices (replacement cost) and exit-from-the-market prices (realisable value or opportunity cost).

Future values are predictive in that they look to the estimated future cash stream and discount this to present value, using a discount factor appropriate to the entity's borrowing rate and also to the considered element of uncertainty – that is, risk – associated with the prediction.

Another way of categorising those values is to look to the markets on which they are based, and this is the approach adopted by Hendriksen.[14] An entity operates in two types of market – the market in which it buys and the market in which it sells. Thus there are input values and output values. The former reflect a measure of what has been given up to obtain the assets for use; the latter reflect the funds expected to be received in the future, based on the exchange price for the entity's product.

The (past) historical cost and (current) replacement cost bases represent input values, while the (current) realisable value and (future) discounted value bases represent output values.

Valuation and capital maintenance

Before we proceed, it may be useful to emphasise the clear distinction between the evalution of resources which represent capital and the maintenance of this capital. They are not one and the same thing. The evaluation of resources is necessary, using one of the three bases available, so that the amount of capital can be computed at (say) two different points in time. The change in the amount of capital forms the basis of the measurement of income. To this change in capital is then applied a charge for the maintenance of capital, using whichever concept is favoured. But this concept of maintenance may differ from the valuation basis used. Having maintained the capital, the remaining amount of movement represents the gain (or loss) for the period.

For example, resources may be evaluated based on the cost to replace them. Having quantified the amount of capital represented by these resources, the contributors of this capital may decide that they wish to maintain its spending power as measured by the change in a consumer index for the period. In determining the income for the period, therefore, a (maintenance of capital) charge computed using the consumer index will be made. This will prevent any indicated deterioration of capital on this basis from being distributed as if it were income.

Income measurement and asset replacement

The issue of providing for the replacement of assets appears to be inextricably linked with any discussion of the measurement of income. A common criticism of the historical cost income model, for example, is that in times of rising prices the series of depreciation amounts charged for the use of an asset does not, in aggregate, ensure sufficient retentions to enable the asset eventually to be replaced. (This point is demonstrated at Chapter 3 in measuring historical cost income using the basic data given at Chapter 1.)

It must be emphasised at this stage that providing for asset replacement and measuring income are quite separate issues. If, for example, the concept of capital is original money capital – that is, historical cost capital – it is entirely proper that the measurement of historical cost income concerns only the depreciation of the original cost of an asset over the period of its useful service. This is the recognition of the consumption of service potential. If the price of the asset remains stable throughout its useful life, then, as a secondary issue, the amounts charged against income for its consumption will aggregate the amount needed for its eventual replacement.[15]

The same issue is encountered in the discussion of replacement cost accounting (see Chapter 5) and backlog depreciation. There are two points which should be made here. Firstly, replacement cost accounting implies nothing about the intentions of management to replace a particular asset. Replacement of specific assets is an investment issue, while the replacement cost approach is simply a basis of asset valuation and/or a concept of capital.

Secondly, backlog depreciation arises because of price movements of an asset subsequent to the depreciation charge against income in any period being made. If this depreciation is not charged against income, insufficient funds could be retained for the asset's eventual replacement. Yet not charging this backlog depreciation against income is a fair treatment which recognises that the replacement of assets is a separate, albeit important, issue from the measurement of income.

Income measurement and distribution policy

A further area of potential confusion is distribution policy. If income is defined as the amount which may be distributed for a period while not impairing the capital with which the business started, this may appear to imply that the income can be paid out as dividend.

This does not necessarily follow. Firstly, the concept of capital which is followed in measuring income is only a means of determining that measurement; for example, the historical cost income model adopts original money capital as the amount which has to be preserved but, in times of rising prices, it probably would be folly to distribute all the income measured on this basis. There would be insufficient left from which to finance the continued operation of the business on the same physical scale without resorting to (ever increasing) borrowings.

This takes us to the second point. The measurement of income necessarily assumes that the capital to be maintained, however defined, is static; that is, that expansion and contraction of the business are not relevant considerations. While this may be valid for measuring income, it is not necessarily a realistic assumption in determining distribution policy. If, for example, the business wishes to expand operations and to finance this expansion wholly or partly from income, this same income cannot be distributed to the proprietors. Equally if the business wishes to contract its operations, then not only can all its income be distributed but also that part of capital which represents the extent of the contraction.

This common feature in the life of businesses – expansion or contraction and the impact on distribution policy – was well recognised, for example, by the stillborn Exposure Draft No 18 "Current Cost Accounting".[16] This proposed that income, once measured (in this case on a mixed value basis), be transferred to an "appropriation account". This account was intended to provide the opportunity for management to address issues such as expansion and contraction and to "tune" the amount measured as income to what they considered prudently distributable.

Even if it is considered prudent to distribute all income earned it does not follow, other than in exceptional cases, that the cash resources are available to fund the distribution; this is the third point. Often specific borrowing has to be introduced for this purpose because the increment to wealth, representing the income earned, is manifested in less liquid resources such as inventories, debtors and property, plant and equipment. Liquidity, therefore, can have a significant impact on distribution policy, regardless of profitability.

General inflation and the unstable measurement unit

So far we have assumed that the monetary unit used to weight the assets in a common expression has a stable, constant value (or purchasing power) through time. This would mean that all changes to asset prices were due to the influences of specific markets only. But the problem with this measurement unit – money – is that it is also used as a medium of exchange – that is, to buy and sell goods and services. As a consequence it is subject to macro- and micro-economic pressures which cause its value, or purchasing power, to fluctuate over time. Examples of such pressures are the supply and velocity of money compared with the supply of goods and services available in the economy and price changes to basic commodities. This fluctuation, or general changes to prices, is usually termed general inflation (or deflation).

It is in times of general inflation that the assumption of a stable monetary unit if manifestly false. If general inflation over a period has been (say) 100%, the general purchasing power of the monetary unit will have halved; the unit can only buy half the amount of a given parcel of goods and services that it could at the beginning of the period. Sweeney put it this way:

> The success of the whole system of business depends upon the truthfulness of reports. The truthfulness of reports depends mainly upon the truthfulness of accounting. The truthfulness of accounting depends largely upon the truthfulness of the dollar – and the dollar is a liar! For it says one thing and means another.[17]

When there is general inflation, the movement in net wealth measured by deducting opening capital from closing capital involves the use of a measuring unit when the value of this is unstable. This is misleading because the lack of comparability of the opening and closing amounts means that the movement is distorted. It is as if the opening and closing capital have been evaluated in different currencies.

Thus, in times of general inflation, there are two types of price change. The first, the general or inflationary change, reflects general inflation which tends to affect the prices of most goods and services to a greater or lesser degree. The second is the specific price change which reflects changes in specific goods and services caused, for example, by technological development or obsolescence, changing tastes, and speculation.

Additionally there may be the considered influence of general price changes on specific prices. This is the derived or relative price change, determined by firstly taking account of general price changes. Once the general change has been accounted for, the remainder reflects the change in one good or service relative to others (sometimes referred to as the "real" change). Thus, general and relative price changes are reflected in specific price changes, although it may be difficult to separate them into their constituent parts in most instances. If there is no general inflation, all price changes are both all specific and all relative.

The duality of use of the monetary unit – as a measuring unit and as a medium of exchange – is only fully reconcilable in the ideal, and unrealistic, perfect world of no general price changes. This has given rise to suggestions that a separate measurement unit – the purchasing power unit – be used to assist in the measurement of income.

The Sandilands Committee was strongly against using units of purchasing power as the measurement unit. It suggested five principal criteria which the measurement unit should have:

(1) equally useful to all users
(2) no change from year to year
(3) the same for all enterprises
(4) preferably a physical object exchangeable by users
(5) of a constant value through time[18]

It then went on to conclude that the monetary unit met the first four criteria[19] while the purchasing power unit met only criterion 5, and even at that "very imperfectly". It went on to say:

> In our opinion a unit of measurement with an absolute value through time is unattainable, and the search for such a unit is illusory. We see no advantage in drawing up accounts in current purchasing power units rather than in units of money.[20]

Further, it considered the split between "inflation" and "real" gains to be "meaningless":

> It is misleading to assume that the movement in some wide-ranging specific index such as the RPI can approximate to the rate of inflation in the abstract and, for example, that if the price of a commodity increases by 100 per cent during a period when the RPI increases by 20 per cent, that 20 per cent of the price increase is due to inflation and 80 per cent is due to other factors. To an individual purchasing this commodity such a distinction has no practical meaning.[21]

None the less there are many respected authorities who see a use for the purchasing power unit, either in a comprehensive system of capital maintenance or simply as a means of segregating inflationary gains from "real" gains.

The classification of gains

Having determined "real" gains, further questions arise. There are three which should be considered:

(1) why should the constituents of gains be separately classified?
(2) what are the constituents?
(3) which constituents can be classified as income?

In trying to answer the first question it is often held that identifying the separate reasons for gains assists in the making of decisions; the split between causes due to effective management and to good luck is considered particularly relevant, for example, by Hendriksen.[22] In an aggregate view of an entity's entire lifespan the analysis of gains is of secondary importance because, having taken inflationary gains to one side, the remainder are all increases to the entity's wealth. Given the emphasis on periodic reporting, as discussed earlier, the analysis assumes much more importance because of the need to take decisions about the future.

In response to the second question, the constituents are usually categorised as holding gains, operating gains and extraordinary gains. Holding gains represent the increment arising from holding an asset during a period when the price increases; they are thus price-related. They can be conveniently classified into three sub-headings for business assets: inventory, those relating to long-term assets which are depreciated, such as plant, and those relating to other long-term assets which are not depreciated, such as land. Another way of looking at them is to consider them cost savings made by purchasing an asset at a point when the price was lower. It is this gain, which includes any gain due to general inflation, which is usually fed automatically into the computation of historical cost income during a period of rising prices, thereby – so the opponents of this concept would argue – obscuring both "real" gains and "real" operating income. If disclosed separately, holding gains can represent an important indication of buying performance for an entity.

Operating gains arise from the production of a quantity of goods and/or services; they therefore relate to quantities, not to price. As McDonald has pointed out, in a global view wealth can be increased only when there is an increase in the quantities of goods and services available (production or operating gains); in contrast, prices reflect the ratios in which the goods and services are available for exchanges, and changes to prices (holding gains) only affect the distribution of the existing aggregate wealth among individuals or firms.[23]

The classification as extraordinary gains is more arbitrary and nebulous. The essence appears to be any gain which is not part of an entity's normal operation and which is also, possibly, non-recurring.[24]

A further division of gains can be made into those realised and unrealised. In considering holding gains a realised gain can be considered one where the asset in question has been disposed of in the period; conversely the gain is unrealised if the asset is still held at the end of the period. Gains equivalent to depreciation charges are treated as realised because the depreciation costs have been charged, and so recognised, in the statement of income, indicating that any benefit has already been enjoyed.

Realisation of revenue and expenses is dependent on a number of criteria; recognition in the statement of income follows realisation. Actual realisation into cash may come later and usually is not relevant for this purpose. Having recognised the revenue the related expenses are also recognised under the accruals or matching concept. Revenue recognition and accruals are discussed in more detail below. It follows that in all models, other than the economic income model, operating and extraordinary gains reported in the income statement must be considered realised.

Having classified the gains into holding, operating and extraordinary, and the holding gains further into realised and unrealised, we can proceed to the third question: which constituents of total gains can be validly classified as income? Operating and extraordinary gains present no problem; they are clearly income. The treatment of holding gains, however, is by no means certain. It depends substantially on the concept of capital, on its maintenance and, therefore, on the income model preferred. If, for example, capital represents operating capacity at replacement cost, then the relevant income is operating income, and holding gains form no part of it. This is the line, for example, followed by the Sandilands Committee.[25] Alternatively, if the replacement cost capital is regarded as a money value, there may be a case for including any holding gains in income.[26]

Under the realisable value view of capital no distinction is considered necessary and in any case can be difficult. "Holding gains", more accurately thought of as non-trading gains under this system, form part of income.[27] The historical income model usually treats some holding gains, such as those on inventories, as income and others, such as those on land, as direct additions to capital.

The final point about the classification of gains as income was touched on by the reference earlier to extraordinary items: namely, which approach is taken to the inclusion of revenue and expenses in income – the current operating approach or the all-inclusive approach? Proponents of the former view advocate that the concentration of attention on events of the current period give a better, more useful indication of a firm's progress because it reflects on matters that are controllable by management and, if financial analysts and commentators are going to emphasise one figure only for income, it is better if it is the current operating income. Thus, events relating to a prior period should be excluded and there should be an emphasis on normal activities.

Proponents of the all-inclusive approach argue that all events of whatever period should be reported as they become known, before period income is determined. They say that the current income approach is too arbitrary in many of the judgments required, is exposed to manipulation and that many of the decisions affecting employees and long-term assets such as plant were taken by management in prior periods, thereby calling into question the integrity of the term "current operating profit".

Realisation, recognition and allocation

Criteria for revenue to be considered as realised and the timing of the recognition of revenue are fundamental to the discussion of any income model. The starting point, for example, for the historical cost income measurement is the recognition of trading revenues. Expense is then allocated to related revenue-producing operations, either current or future, using the accruals or matching concept. In the absence of any demonstrable link to confidently expected future benefits, expense is allocated to the time period in which it was incurred. Thus, income is measured as the difference between revenues recognised and allocated historical costs. It can be seen, therefore, that the judgments related to revenue recognition and cost allocation are of prime importance in determining historical cost income. McDonald put it this way:

> Revenue is the independent variable while expenses are a quasi-dependent variable and net income is entirely a dependent variable. Revenue is measured entirely independently from considerations of expenses or the resulting net income. In contrast, expenses are usually measured in terms of the revenues to which they are related through the application of the matching concept. Finally income emerges through the summing of the revenues and the expenses which are at least partially a function of those revenues. Thus the concept of revenue is basic to the present methods by which income is measured.[28]

The terms "recognition" and "realised" are often used in discussing revenue. Throughout this text revenue is "recognised" when it appears in the income statement at a measured amount; it is "realised" at the point in time when it is considered appropriate to measure it. Both, of course, determine the timing of revenue reporting, which is important for the periodic measurement of income but not for the absolute answer – it all comes to the same result once the transaction is complete.

There are many bases of revenue realisation and recognition which can be followed and these can be categorised as transactions-based, activities-based or as something in between. The former is much the more commonly encountered in historical cost accounting; for example, realisation may be said to have occurred at the point of shipment of the goods or issue of the invoice or at each of several points of the invoices being issued where there are instalment sales. Transactions-based realisation usually involves the transformation of assets from one form – say, inventories – to another – say, debtors or cash. One of the arguments used by those who adopt this basis is the practicality of being able to measure revenue with near certainty.

This can be in contrast to activities-based realisation, which is less common under historical cost accounting but quite likely using, for example, a current cash equivalent model. Relative certainty may be forfeited for economic realism by adopting the idea, for example, that the process of earning revenue covers several, or many, facets of a firm's operations and that it is incorrect to delay realisation until, for example, delivery of the goods. As Hendriksen points out, the value added by a productive activity is a continuous process and it is the uncertainty over the expected amount of future revenue to be received subsequently which has given rise to arbitrary rules for the historical cost model. He quotes Sprouse & Moonitz:

> Revenues should be identified during which the major economic activities necessary to the creation and disposition of goods and services have been accomplished, provided objective measurements of the results of those activities are available. These two conditions, *ie*, accomplishment of major economic activity and objectivity of measurement, are fulfilled at different

stages of activity in different cases, sometimes as late as time of delivery of product or the performance of a service, in other cases, at an earlier point of time.[29]

Hendriksen goes on to discuss an expedient to overcome the practical difficulties of implementing continuous revenue recognition. This is to base realisation on the critical event. The single most appropriate event in the revenue-generating process is selected. This might be when the most difficult task is completed; for example, when a contract is signed.

In all, five approaches are discussed, covering both the transactions and activities bases: the reporting of revenue during production, including long-term contracts; accretion, as in growing timber or whisky maturing; at completion of production, if there is a firm contract for the sale of the product; at the time of sale; and subsequent to sale where, for example, it is not possible to estimate the amount of revenue which has been generated at the time of sale, such as in an exchange for non-monetary assets.

Expenses allocation

Among the most difficult expenses to allocate are those related to inventories and depreciation on long-term (fixed) assets. As Chambers points out, "The valuation of stock and provision for depreciation have long been recognised as the two most complex problems in accounting".[30] (He then goes on to explain how changing price levels have made these problems even more complex.) The multiplicity of methods, often arbitrary, of allocating costs in these areas would tend to support this statement. Consider, for example, the choice of first in – first out, last in – first out, and next in – first out, etc, in the allocation of inventories' expense and the complexities involved in the allocation of overhead expenses; again consider depreciation methods such as straight-line, reducing balance, sum of the digits, double declining, and so on, and the actual depreciation rates employed. Other areas of cost allocation, such as deferred tax, pension costs and research and development costs, also can have a highly significant effect on how income is measured.

Usefulness and supporting characteristics and constraints

Whatever bases and methods are used to measure income, the end product must be useful. Usefulness, that is, being good information for the user and for the purpose in mind, is generally perceived to be the key characteristic of all financial statements. Like all characteristics, usefulness relates to both the measurement concept adopted and the presentation of the outcome of this measurement. Many commentaries have been written on the supporting qualitative characteristics or constraints which are needed to achieve the goal of usefulness and on the requirements of the law for a defined quality of information (see, for example, Flint's discussion in "A True and Fair View in Company Accounts"[31]). While a full discussion of these characteristics is outside the scope of this text, it may be helpful to list those which usually feature.

(*a*) *Relevance* To be useful, data must be measured and reported in a way which is relevant to the user. Hence, for example, data which is immaterial in amount and nature need not be highlighted, thereby giving emphasis to information which is significant. Chambers considers relevance the single most significant characteristic.[32] Both Sterling[33] and Lee[34] regard it as the principal support to usefulness in measuring income. In a study of theory published in 1966 the American Accounting Association stressed particularly the importance of relevance.[35] The fundamental difficulty with relevance, however, is the underlying presumption that those preparing accounting information are aware of the information which the user wants or needs.

(*b*) *Realism* The information reported should be realistic; that is, it must reflect, and relate to, real world circumstances. This is one of Sterling's principal requirements (he calls it verity) along with relevance.[36]

(*c*) *Objectivity; freedom from bias* Objectivity here means freedom from bias; that is, the information being reported should be neutral in that the measurement should not be biased towards any single group of competing user interests. In Accounting Research Study No. 1, by Moonitz, it was expressed as one of the basic postulates:

> Postulate C-2, Objectivity. Changes in assets and liabilities, and the related effects (if any) on revenues, expenses, retained earnings, and the like, should not be given formal recognition in the accounts earlier than the point of time at which they can be measured in objective terms.[37]

(*d*) *Reliability; verifiability* Information is considered to have greater value if it has been possible to verify it independently or confirm aspects of it. However, as Hendriksen has pointed out,[38] some care is needed here. It is one thing to verify facts – such as the cost of plant bought some time ago; it is another to interpret this as the best indication (say) of current value today. The interpretation is not free from bias, although the underlying fact can be verified.

(*e*) *Comparability* To be useful, information reported about one period's activities should be expressed in a way which makes it easier to compare with another period; likewise information between entities should be expressed in comparable terms to the extent that the information is, in fact, comparable. Chambers is particularly keen on comparability:

> The greater the consistency of uses of methods of allocation the greater

> will be the comparability of successive statements. No possibility of alternatives at the discretion of the record keeper can be admitted. Nor can any procedure be admitted which is consistently biased in any direction. Nor can any external change which induces internal changes in a period or over successive periods be disregarded; for the impact of external changes will differ from period to period (the environment being fluid) destroying the comparability of successive statements. Comparability is not to be understood as similarity in size of results or effects; any device selected because this will be its effect operates to defeat the purpose of reporting and is inconsistent with the service function of the record. The very purpose of comparison is to discern the sizes of changes or deviations.[39]

Consistency in the application of like methods for like circumstances assists comparability, but only where the choice is between methods of equal relevance. Blind mechanical application of a method which is not the most appropriate treatment simply results in distorted information being reported. As the Trueblood Committee most aptly put it, "The desire for consistency should not become an obsession that impedes progress".[40]

(*f*) *Understandability* There is little point in presenting data if it is unlikely to be understood. It should be clear and understandable without being simplistic. This is similar to the materiality concept in that trivial data should not be highlighted, thereby reducing the chance of confusion. The Sandilands Report perhaps offers a useful comment:

> We accept as an overall objective that accounts should be as simple as possible. However, brevity is not always synonymous with clarity. It is illusory to expect that "the true position" of a major industrial or commercial group can be shown by a small number of figures on a single sheet of paper. The operations of such groups are complex, and their accounts will necessarily also be complex. This does not mean that they cannot be clear and comprehensible, if they are based on well-defined and logical principles.[41]

There has also been fairly recent research to suggest that, for example, financial statements presented to shareholders are not well understood.[42]

(*g*) *Timeliness* Information should be presented which is current; that is, if the information relates to current or relatively recent measures of value, these may be considered more relevant than older indications of value. Again timely presentation of data – that is, as soon as possible after it had been prepared – is more useful and relevant for making predictions and decisions than dated information.

It can be seen that relevance and realism appear to be the principal supporting criteria to achieve usefulness. The other remaining characteristics are really practical expedients which support relevance and realism; they also tend to modify them in some circumstances.

Hendriksen has usefully categorised these sub-goals into user constraints and measurement constraints.[43] User constraints are those which respond to the needs and limitations of the user; thus materiality (supporting relevance), comparability (and its support, consistency), and timeliness are put into this category. While not specifically considered by Hendriksen, understandability would also be a user constraint. Measurement constraints reflect the limitations of available data and the effect of the environment on the accuracy and reliability of measurements; objectivity and reliability are examples.

The foregoing list is not, of course, exhaustive. For example, in Statement of Standard Accounting Practice No 2[44] there are identified and described four fundamental "concepts" – namely, going concern, accruals, consistency (already discussed) and prudence. The going concern, or continuity, idea is that an economic enterprise will continue in existence into the foreseeable future in the absence of evidence to the contrary. The concept underpins the deferment of costs being charged in the measurement of income – for example, the carrying forward of fixed asset costs to future operating periods. There is dispute about whether this foreseeable future is that which is sufficient to carry out existing commitments or, in effect, perpetuity because new commitments are usually made before completion of old and unrelated ones, thereby prolonging continuity indefinitely.

Sterling argues that it is misleading to make continuity an assumption and that it is more in the nature of a prediction[45] but that, in any case, it is not necessary to adopt the idea to allow costs to be taken forward to a future period (a definite life can justify this).[46] In referring to Sterling's views Lee adds that the continuity argument has been adopted by accountants because it can be used to justify the exclusion of unrealised value changes, which suits a conservative and cautious outlook and helps to justify the historical cost system.[47]

The alternative to going concern is discontinuation, which gives rise to quite different valuation and measurement bases. As we shall see later, however, the going concern idea, in its application to concepts of income measurement, is not universally accepted as relevant (see Chapter 6 and the discussion of current cash equivalents).

The accruals idea is a means of trying to impute realism to economic events which relate to incomplete transactions; that is, the cycle of possessing cash, investing it in various activities and materials, adding value, and converting all this back to cash is incomplete. Thus the question of when revenue should be recognised is a problem of applying the accruals concept; there is a general belief that revenue should be recognised as it is "earned" (but this begs the question, which was discussed above, of when revenue is earned). Likewise the matching of related costs incurred adopts the accruals concept because, again, the transactions cycle concerned with costs may not have been completed.

Clearly this idea can conflict with conservatism and, in the UK when this happens, conservatism (prudence) takes precedence.[48] The matching concept may have more relevance to those primarily interested in income measurement, while those concerned about security of capital or loans may favour emphasis on conservatism. Expenses recognition can be based on transactions or activities. Those which are activities-based can be matched with the recognition of the related revenue. However, in practice, this is not always easy; the result is the (conservative) rule that, in the absence of any justifiable link between expenses and revenue, the expenses should be allocated against the revenue of the period in which they are incurred; that is, they become transactions-based. Thus, for example, expenses incurred on raw materials consumed in the manufacture of goods would be matched against revenue as and when the latter was realised and recognised; in contrast, salaries expense of a personnel department may be difficult to link to specific revenue, in which case it would be charged against the period in which it had been incurred. These are two fairly clear examples, but there are many more which fall into the grey area between revenue and period expenses.

Matching expenses to revenue means that recognition of these expenses in the income statement will be deferred until the revenue is deemed realised and recognised. Should this transcend reporting periods where, for example, the historical cost or replacement cost income models are adopted, the expenses will be shown in the balance sheet listed among the captions of assets. However, the positive correlation that is needed to justify the matching of costs to revenue can often be elusive in practice, with the consequent danger that arbitrariness will be adopted as a (meaningless?) surrogate for demonstrable correlation. Gilman defines assets (in the historical cost system) as cash and claims to cash, both immediate (such as bank accounts) and deferred (such as debtors), and deferred charges to future revenue (such as inventories, plant and buildings and prepaid expenses).[49]

The fourth concept advanced by SSAP 2 is the prudence concept. Revenue and profit are neither anticipated nor recognised until realised into cash or until such realisation "can be assessed with reasonable certainty". All known liabilities (expenses and losses) should be provided for. This rather cautious approach is particularly sourced in the transaction basis of historical cost accounting.

Originally it was adopted in the nineteenth century, when potential lenders to owner-managed firms preferred a cautious approach to asset valuation because it provided extra cover by tending to restrict the loan. Over time it came to be abused in some quarters in a preoccupation with pessimism. It has run into much criticism because, it is argued, it has caused distortion of information by over-zealous application.

Barton summarises the applications of it today as the creation of "secret" reserves by:

(1) inconsistent application of the realisation concept; for example, contrast the rather late revenue recognition of the historical cost model with early expenses recognition
(2) overstatement of expenses; for example, by anticipating those in the future or by accelerated depreciation allocation
(3) write-off of long-term intangible assets as quickly as income will permit
(4) bias in estimates of doubtful debtors and liabilities such as tax.

By creating "secret" reserves, he concludes, there is then much greater scope for "income smoothing"; that is, the manipulation of reported income so that a relatively smooth upward trend is shown rather than what may be the more factual, and volatile, picture.[50] The problem here is obvious. A "managed" trend may lead users to incorrect predictions and decisions.

Hendriksen is also highly critical of the application of prudence:

> The term "conservatism" is generally used to mean that accountants should report the lowest of several possible values for assets and revenues and the highest of several possible values for liabilities and expenses. It also implies that expenses should be recognized sooner rather than later and that revenues should be recognized later rather than sooner. Therefore, net assets are more likely to be valued below current exchange prices rather than above, and the computation of income is likely to result in the lowest of several alternative amounts. Thus, pessimism is assumed to be better than optimism in financial reporting.[51]

He points out that its application conflicts with the objective to present all relevant information.[52]

While these may be strong criticisms, the application of conservatism requires a value judgment about an uncertain future from each person who tries to apply it, and it is extremely difficult to standardise an approach to it. The problem, therefore, is not about the concept of being reasonably certain but rather about the abuse in its application. *The Corporate Report* points out that prudence is useful, for example to loan creditors, in assessing economic stability and vulnerability.[53]

Of the four concepts it can be seen that two are questioned for their relevance (going concern and prudence) and two can be seen as sub-goals of the earlier characteristics; accruals is a sub-goal of realism and consistency a sub-goal of comparability.

Summary

These two introductory chapters, in setting the scene for the rest of the text, have sought to indicate that:

(1) the essence of accounting is the measurement of stocks of resources and flows from these stocks; measurement is the process of applying weights (prices) to heterogeneous resources and events of an economic nature which were quantified originally by various disparate measures;

(2) the measurement, and especially the periodic measurement, of the income flow is in demand;

(3) the difficulty peculiar to periodic measurement of income is the assessment of incomplete transactions and events and, therefore, the valuation of non-cash assets;

(4) income is the increase in net wealth (or welloffness) after adjustment for further contributions by, and distributors to, proprietors and, hence, opening capital must be maintained before income can be said to have accrued;

(5) to measure the increase in net wealth and, therefore, income there are four fundamental and distinct stages –

   (a) identifying resources or assets, their qualities and their quantities,

   (b) selecting the measurement property of the monetary unit to be adopted from a choice of either monetary units or purchasing power units,

   (c) selecting the valuation basis of the assets (*ie*, the measurement weightings to be applied to the quantities) from a choice of four principal bases:

      (i) historical cost
      (ii) replacement cost } input values

      (iii) realisable value
      (iv) present discounted value; } output values

   (d) selecting the concept of capital to be maintained before income can be determined, from a choice of four principal concepts:

      (i) original shareholders' capital
      (ii) replacement capital
      (iii) current cash equivalent capital } in either money or purchasing power terms
      (iv) economic capital;

(6) income can be classified into operating and extraordinary gains; holding gains, both inflationary and relative, and realised and unrealised, may also be included in income depending upon the concept of capital which is preferred; and

(7) the paramount objective in making a choice from the options available in measuring income is usefulness of the information to the user; to be

achieved, usefulness needs to be supported by many qualitative characteristics, of which relevance and realism are primary.

Perceived usefulness will vary by type of user (and perhaps by user within type) and no one single concept of income, therefore, will be the most useful for every purpose. Sandilands, in considering the varying and sometimes conflicting requirements of users, explained it thus:

> The range of possible information of the activities of companies that could be shown in accounting statements is so large that for practical reasons priorities have to be selected, and accounting practices established which as far as possible lead to the disclosure of information useful to all those who are likely to use company accounts. Users of accounts may be classified into certain groups, but their requirements for information may not be the same, nor are they likely to regard certain types of information as equally important.[54]

The key measurements, or variables, in the measurement of income have been identified above as:

- the measurement property of the monetary unit
- the asset valuation basis
- the concept of capital
- the classification of holding gains (which is part of the concept of capital but sufficiently important to identify separately).

Succeeding chapters discuss the six principal income models available using these key variables as reference points for comparison and contrast. The simple cxample given in the Prologue is used throughout to demonstrate the income model in use.

References and notes

1. I. Fisher, *The Theory of Interest*, Macmillan, 1930, Chapter 1.
2. J. R. Hicks, *Value and Capital*, Clarendon Press, 1946, page 172.
3. E. S. Hendriksen, *Accounting Theory* (3rd edition), Richard D. Irwin Inc, 1982, page 144.
4. F. E. P. Sandilands, "Inflation Accounting". Report of the Inflation Accounting Committee, HMSO, 1975, page 29.
5. Ibid, page 161.
6. "Accounting for the Effects of Changing Prices", Exposure Draft 35, Accounting Standards Committee, 1984; and "Current Cost Accounting", Statement of Standard Accounting Practice No 16, Accounting Standards

Committee, 1980. [ED 35 is unlikely to be universally accepted and may well be revised in the future.]

7. See, for example, Statement of Financial Accounting Standards No 33 by the Financial Accounting Standards Board, 1979 (USA); Statement of Accounting Practice No 1 by Institute of Chartered Accountants in Australia and the Australian Society of Accountants, 1983 (Australia); CCA Standard No 1 by the New Zealand Society of Accountants, 1982 (New Zealand).
8. R. J. Chambers, *Accounting, Evaluation and Economic Behaviour*, Prentice-Hall, 1966, page 103.
9. D. L. McDonald, *Comparative Accounting Theory*, Addison-Wesley, 1972, page 93.
10. J. B. Canning, *The Economics of Accountancy*, Ronald Press, 1929, page 22.
11. E. S. Hendriksen, *Accounting Theory*, pages 257 and 258.
12. D. L. McDonald, *Comparative Accounting Theory*, page 62.
13. Y. Ijiri, *The Foundations of Accounting Measurement*, Prentice-Hall, 1967, Chapter 4.
14. E. S. Hendriksen, *Accounting Theory*, page 264.
15. Such depreciation charges can breed what W. T. Baxter calls "secondary assets" in his monograph *Depreciating Assets*, published for The Institute of Chartered Accountants of Scotland by Gee/Van Nostrand Reinhold (UK) in 1981 (page 9). As he points out, so long as the owners take the income measurement seriously, depreciation charges will mean smaller dividends thereby leading to conservation of funds; these funds can be invested in other assets, such as more stocks or other depreciating assets.
16. "Current Cost Accounting", Exposure Draft No 18. Accounting Standards Committee, 1976.
17. H. W. Sweeney, *Stabilized Accounting*, Harper & Row, 1936, page xi.
18. F. E. P. Sandilands, "Inflation Accounting". Report of the Inflation Accounting Committee, page 43.
19. *Ibid.*, page 57.
20. *Ibid.*, page 123.
21. *Ibid.*, page 13.
22. E. S. Hendriksen, *Accounting Theory*, page 127.
23. D. L. McDonald, *Comparative Accounting Theory*, page 98.
24. See, for example, "Extraordinary Items and Prior Year Adjustments", Statement of Standard Accounting Practice No 6, Accounting Standards Committee, 1974, and "Extraordinary Items", Accounting Principles Board Opinion No 30: American Institute of Certified Public Accountants, 1973.
25. F. E. P. Sandilands, "Inflation Accounting", Report of the Inflation Accounting Committee, page 141.
26. See, for example, T. A. Lee, *Income and Value Measurement* (2nd edition), Van Nostrand Reinhold (UK), 1980, page 85.

27. See, for example, A. D. Barton, *The Anatomy of Accounting* (2nd edition), University of Queensland Press, 1977, page 386.
28. D. L. McDonald, *Comparative Accounting Theory*, page 99.
29. E. S. Hendriksen, *Accounting Theory*, page 181.
30. R. J. Chambers, "Accounting and Shifting Price Levels", *The Australian Accountant*, September 1949; re-printed in *Accounting Finance and Management*, Butterworths, 1969, page 295.
31. D. Flint, *A True and Fair View in Company Accounts*. A monograph of The Institute of Chartered Accountants of Scotland, Gee/Van Nostrand Reinhold (UK), 1980.
32. R. J. Chambers, "Blueprint for a Theory of Accounting", *Accounting Research*, January 1955. Re-printed in *Accounting, Finance and Management*, page 347.
33. R. R. Sterling, *The Theory and Measurement of Enterprise Income*, The University Press of Kansas, 1970, page 40.
34. T. A. Lee, *Income and Value Measurement*, page 24.
35. The American Accounting Association, *A Statement of Basic Accounting Theory*.
36. R. R. Sterling, *The Theory and Measurement of Enterprise Income*, page 40.
37. M. Moonitz, "The Basic Postulates of Accounting", Accounting Research Study No 1. American Institute of Certified Public Accountants, 1961, page 53.
38. E. S. Hendriksen, *Accounting Theory*, page 129.
39. R. J. Chambers, "Towards a General Theory of Accounting", 1961; reprinted in *Accounting, Finance and Management*, page 502.
40. R. M. Trueblood, "Objectives of Financial Statements", Report of The Study Group on the Objectives of Financial Statements, AICPA, 1973, page 60.
41. F. E. P. Sandilands, "Inflation Accounting", Report of the Inflation Accounting Committee, page 65.
42. T. A. Lee and D. P. Tweedie, "The Private Shareholder and the Corporate Report", The Institute of Chartered Accountants in England and Wales, 1977.
43. E. S. Hendriksen, *Accounting Theory*, pages 120–130.
44. "Dislosure of Accounting Policies", Statement of Standard Accounting Practice No 2, Accounting Standards Committee, 1971.
45. R. R. Sterling, "Elements of Pure Accounting Theory", *Accounting Review*, January 1967, pages 62–73.
46. A similar argument is made by R. R. Sterling in *Conservatism: the Fundamental Principle of Valuation in Traditional Accounting*, *Abacus*, December 1967, page 110.

47. T. A. Lee, *Income and Value Measurement*, page 57.
48. See "Disclosure of Accounting Policies", Statement of Standard Accounting Practice No 2, Accounting Standards Committee, 1971.
49. S. Gilman, *Accounting Concepts of Profit*, Ronald Press, 1939, page 300.
50. A. D. Barton, *The Anatomy of Accounting*, pages 299–303.
51. E. S. Hendriksen, *Accounting Theory*, page 132.
52. *Ibid.*, page 134.
53. "The Corporate Report". A discussion paper by the Accounting Standards Committee, 1975, page 65.
54. F. E. P. Sandilands, "Inflation Accounting", Report of the Inflation Accounting Committee, page 16.

3 The Historical Cost Income Model

Brief history

Historical cost accounting remains the most common system today for recording and reporting accounting information. Sometimes referred to as "conventional" or "traditional" accounting, it has been around since at least the sixteenth century and perhaps earlier. The present characteristics were developed in the nineteenth and early twentieth centuries when there was a considerable growth in the company with limited liability. This created a need for more widely available financial information although, initially, since this need came principally from creditors, the emphasis was on the statement of resources or balance sheet. The more that businesses came to be financed and owned by outsiders and the less that they were owner-managed the greater the demand there was for financial information on a periodic basis. The gradually increasing importance of periodic information in the 1920s and 1930s, together with the developing emphasis on profit as a corporate tax base, promoted the income statement to prominence and relegated the balance sheet to a rather lowly position of presenting residual balances.

Basis of accounting

The basis of historical cost accounting, and the financial statements which rely on this basis, is acquisition cost – that is, the exchange price or sacrifice at the time the transaction involving the resource originally took place. This arises from the fundamental feature of all accounting, of recording and stating basic inputs in the monetary amounts at the date of each transaction.

Hence the historical cost system is transactions-based – that is, changes in valuations of assets and liabilities are only recorded following transactions (or realisations), including internal transactions such as the conversion of raw materials to finished goods. In practice, market changes are sometimes recognised. For example, the lower of cost and net realisable value rule is followed in pricing inventory, although this is a corruption of the pure system and relates to the prudence concept.

The prudence concept plays a significant part in the historical cost system. As already indicated in the previous chapter, this concept was adopted in the nineteenth century when the historical cost system was widely used for stewardship reporting. Some of the criticisms of this model (see later) are related to the use of the prudence concept.

Generally, in the historical cost system revenue realisation and recognition tend to occur late in the production or activity cycle when the outcome is virtually assured. Thus, realisation, in the sense of conversion to cash or financial claims, is a prime feature of historical cost accounting. In the same way holding gains, arising from changes to asset price after acquisition, are usually not recorded until they have been realised.

Matching of expenses to recognised revenue can be effective when there is a clear link with revenue. However, often this link is not demonstrable, with the result that expenses have to be allocated to periods in a more arbitrary way. A good example of the problem of allocation is the spread of depreciation charges of property, plant and equipment over the periods when the use of these assets is estimated to be earning revenue. These and other examples were discussed more fully in Chapter 2.

In fact many of the "assets" shown can be seen as representing costs, the matching of which with revenue has been deferred on some justified basis. These costs may be stated as they were originally incurred or at a remaining unamortised (or unmatched) amount; in either case, to the extent stated, the costs are considered to represent a source of future income flow.

Illustration

Consider an example of historical cost accounting using the data given in the Prologue. The income statements and balance sheets would look like this (all amounts in £s):

	Year				Total
	1	2	3 (before close)	3 (after close)	
INCOME STATEMENT					
Sales	12,000	19,000	23,000		
Purchases and other expenses	(9,000)	(14,000)	(17,000)		
	3,000	5,000	6,000		
Depreciation (£3,900 × 2) ÷ 3	(2,600)	(2,600)	(2,600)		
	400	2,400	3,400		
Gain on sale of property (1)	—	—	—	3,500	
Reported income	400	2,400	3,400	3,500	9,700
BALANCE SHEET					
Property – at cost	8,000	8,000	8,000	—	
Vans – at cost less depreciation (2)	5,200	2,600	—	—	
	13,200	10,600	8,000	—	
Cash (3)	3,000	8,000	14,000	23,500	
Total assets	16,200	18,600	22,000	23,500	
representing –					
Capital (4)					
– original	13,800	13,800	13,800	13,800	
– prior years' profit	—	400	2,800	6,200	
– opening	13,800	14,200	16,600	20,000	
– year's profit	400	2,400	3,400	3,500	
– closing	14,200	16,600	20,000	23,500	
Bank loan	2,000	2,000	2,000	—	
	16,200	18,600	22,000	23,500	

Notes to illustration

(1) At the end of year 3, X sold the property for £11,500. This compares with an original cost of £8,000, giving a historical cost gain of £3,500 which has been included in the statement of income.

(2) Vans – cost at beginning of year 1

Vans – cost at beginning of year 1	£7,800
depreciation charge – year 1	(2,600)
remaining cost – end of year 1	5,200
depreciation charge – year 2	(2,600)
remaining cost – end of year 2	2,600
depreciation charge – year 3	2,600
Remaining cost – end of year 3	—
scrapped; no proceeds	—

(3) Cash represents the operating surplus before depreciation charges. It accumulates each year thus:

Cash from operations – year 1	£3,000
– year 2	5,000
end of year 2	8,000
– year 3	6,000
end of year 3 (before close)	14,000
Cash received from sale of property	11,500
	25,500
Cash paid to eliminate bank loan	(2,000)
	23,500

(4) See discussion of capital concept below.

Measurement property of monetary unit

It can be seen that the measurement property of the monetary unit used is the medium of exchange rather than purchasing power units.

Asset valuation

Assets are either cash or, if representing incomplete transactions, are measured at original prices subject to the allocation of the cost by charges for depreciation, as in the case of vans. This charge is an attempt to spread the cost on a reasonable and systematic basis against the revenue which is created as a result of the vans' use. But this is in the absence of any more specific matching with revenue which can be demonstrated.

The primary purpose of depreciation is the allocation of cost against expected benefit; any other charges to provide for replacement are not truly depreciation but capital maintenance provisions. If the business had continued after year 3 and there had been a need to replace the vans, the depreciation charges of the old vans would have caused enough to have been retained to provide for replacement only if the replacement price had remained the same as the price of the original vans (£7,800) or less, in contrast to the actual cost of replacing the vans at that time (£6,000 × 2 = £12,000). Hence, in conditions of changing prices, the asset measurement basis of historical cost accounting does not assist in the holding back of sufficient resources for replacement. To the extent that there is a deficiency for replacement, capital in a replacement sense has been eroded. Asset replacement was discussed at Chapter 2, where it was explained why it cannot be a factor in measuring income. It should be, however, a significant consideration in determining the policy on the distribution of income.

Concept of capital

The capital maintenance concept of historical cost accounting is the initial monetary investment. So long as the value (that is, cost) of the assets representing the initial monetary investment is recovered against operations, this capital will be maintained. A refinement of the concept is necessary to determine periodic income. This is to express the capital as the monetary value of the proprietor's interest at the beginning of the year. In our example the capital which has to be maintained in year 2 is the original capital of £13,800 and the profit of year 1 (£400). If it were just the £13,800 then the £400 could be classified as part of year 2 income. By including profit in the amount of capital to be preserved in the succeeding period the confusion of distributability with periodic measurement is avoided. Finally, the income of any year can be determined by comparing the opening and closing capital for the year in question.

Classification of holding gains

In line with the cautious prudent approach and transactionism the property holding gain, eventually realised at £3,500 at the end of year 3 is recognised only then but not before. This gain had been building up each year as a glance at the original data at Chapter 1 will demonstrate. The full realised gain has been classified as income because the capital of £8,000 historical cost has been charged in its computation. In practice this type of gain is sometimes classified outside the income statement usually to avoid confusion with operations. Even if treated as a capital gain it is still properly distributable as income under the historical cost capital concept.

A particular influence on the historical cost system has been the legal constraints on the distribution of unrealised gains. This owes much to the historical development of the system and to a conservative view which was influenced much by the perceived need to protect creditors. More recently, in the UK for example, the Companies Act 1981,[1] itself introduced in response to the European Community's Fourth Council Directive of July 1978, specifies that gains considered unrealised cannot be retained in the statement of income and, therefore, they cannot be distributed as income.

The case for the historical cost income model

(1) It is factual and therefore objective.
Comment This is a frequent virtue claimed by proponents. It confuses the factual, objective, inputs of the initial gathering and marshalling process with the outputs in the form of summarised revenues and costs. The many areas have already been discussed where judgment plays a substantial part in determining the timing of what is to be considered realised, the amount to be recognised, the allocation of very significant expenses and the effect of varying individual standards of conservatism.

(2) It is verifiable and this gives the user confidence in the data.
Comment This is true of gross costs but, otherwise, there are the problems of recognition and allocation.

(3) It is understandable.
Comment Users may believe they understand what the data shows but this may be questioned. Again the recognition and allocation problems can undermine the validity of user beliefs, although recognition and allocation rules, applied consistently in succeeding time periods, can alleviate the difficulty.

(4) The basis has stood the test of much time, so that many users must have found it useful.
Comment It may not have stood the test of time; it may simply have survived through default by users' ignorance of alternative systems. The horse was relied on for transport until the locomotive and motor car were developed and people became aware of what each could do.

(5) The system is easier than others to apply because it follows closely the original transaction base which is the input to the underlying record-keeping procedures. This also makes it less costly than other approaches to income measurement.

(6) Following point (5) reconciliation of reported historical cost data with basic records is easy. This means that administrative control is made easier – for example, monitoring-type enquiries.

(7) Because it is transactions-based it is argued that it provides a good report of stewardship and, since the capital to be preserved is the money capital invested, this protects proprietors and creditors alike.
Comment There are two particular arguments against this. The first is the recognition/allocation problem, although it is possible to overstate its validity here. The second relates to what the report of stewardship is really about. Do users interested in stewardship want to know about original money invested and what has happened to this; or are they more concerned with what has happened to the resources of the enterprise in the economic environment in which it has to operate? This is discussed later when considering the case against historical cost accounting.

(8) It is useful as a tax base. Again administrative convenience helps here.

(9) The short-term position, that is, current assets and liabilities, are often shown reasonably accurately because they are either expressed in cash, or near cash terms, or the assets were acquired in the recent past (for example, inventories) and market price at the point of reporting may not be significantly different.
Comment This may be true for those industries with a relatively short trading cycle, but activities like heavy construction, shipbuilding and whisky distilling have a substantial trading cycle which can span several, and sometimes many, years. In such industries inventories can likewise be years old with consequences for the considered relevance of the historical costs at which they are stated.

(10) Historical cost accounting is concerned with the past. It provides a good base, along with other factors, from which to predict the future.

(11) The final point is dependent on stability of the currency (no inflation) and of prices (no

specific changes). If the former condition prevails it is argued that the income measure is particularly useful. In the latter case it is claimed that acquisition costs of assets, in the shorter term, would give a reasonable indication of replacement cost and realisable value.

The case against the historical cost income model

(1) It is not factual and objective. The problems of highly judgmental, often arbitrary, recognition and allocation procedures and of conservatism were referred to earlier. These undermine confidence in the current period's income measurement.
Comment The potential chaos arising is limited by the consistency of treatment of the items in succeeding periods of the same enterprise, although consistency does not extend to treatment of similar items by different enterprises.

(2) If historical cost accounting is not factual it cannot be verifiable. For example, the original cost of a piece of equipment can be verified as can the calculation spreading that cost over several years by depreciation charges. What cannot be verified is the number of years over which it is spread, nor the validity of attempted "matching" in this way with anticipated benefit.

(3) As indicated earlier, true understandability must be in doubt, given the judgmental recognition and allocation difficulties. This applies to two points in particular. The first is the effect which these difficulties can have on periodic reporting of income; because of the emphasis on conservatism prior period revenue recognition may be deferred and current period cost accelerated to the prior period. The choice of options available is very wide. In a stock exchange listed company, for example, this bias tends to favour the prospective buyer against the seller.
The second misunderstanding may be the perception of the balance sheet as an indicator of value when in fact it includes sometimes substantial residual balances following from the allocation decisions that have been made.
Comment This perception, and its inaccuracy, is not confined to the historical cost model.

(4) The remaining arguments against historical cost accounting relate to its usefulness and therefore to its relevance and realism during times of inflation and/or specific price changes. While it can be validly advocated that there are times of almost no general price changes, the same cannot be said for specific price changes. In the absence of inflation all specific changes are relative changes, one good or service to another, in continually changing ratios of perceived value. The main points against the system in times of changing prices (both types) are:
   (a) The income amount will not differentiate between inflationary and "real" gains because the unit of measurement is unstable. This also means that there is no additivity; that is, it is invalid to aggregate assets acquired some time ago with those acquired yesterday because they are expressed in a different currency. Further, the instability causes the trend of periodic results presented to be misleading for the same reason.
   (b) The asset measurement basis is defective and its use, with the capital concept adopted, can result in financial difficulties when the assets are due for replacement. While asset replacement is not a factor in measuring historical cost income, a distribution policy which did not allow sufficient income to be retained could cause replacement difficulties. This can be illustrated simply using our example. If we assume that the business continued and that the income of each year was taken out by X as a distribution to the proprietor, we would find at the beginning of year 4 that

only £7,800 of capital had been preserved when in fact £12,000 was now needed (see Chapter 1). Capital may have been maintained under the historical cost concept of the proprietor's monetary investment, but further capital of £4,200 to continue operations now needs to be injected.
Comment This, of course, is a legitimate choice for the proprietor: whether to inject this or opt for the contraction of the business which its absence represents (or indeed to wind up the business). The same choice faces all proprietors using the historical cost income model in times of rising prices. The question this poses is whether they realise this when, for example, determining distribution policy.

(c) By disregarding changes in asset prices (not recognising holding gains until they are realised) the timeliness of reporting relevant economic events is impaired. Income reported in later periods belonged to earlier periods. By ignoring changes in asset prices the information presented may not give a reliable indication of protection for creditors and of stewardship. The question is really whether up to date indicators of market conditions are more relevant to those for whom an income measurement is primarily a stewardship report, than out of date, but realised, acquisition prices (often made unverifiable by subsequent recognition and allocation judgments).

In terms of achieving usefulness, changing prices, both inflationary and specific, appear to make the historical cost approach to income measurement at best suspect and at worst quite unsatisfactory. There is doubt as to its relevance and therefore usefulness to users in periods of price changes, particularly if these changes are significant. Given that price changes are virtually continual happenings, even if inflation is not, this appears to be a significant defect of historical cost accounting. Businesses which have a short trading cycle, however, may find it acceptable and useful, especially when used with other information such as cash flows.

Historical cost model adapted

The historical cost model discussed thus far has concentrated on its pure application without modification. There are two quite common corruptions of the pure historical cost approach which have developed in an attempt to alleviate the worst effects of price changes on historical cost income measurement. The first is the recording of price changes periodically (holdings gains) on long-term assets, with depreciation charges flexed accordingly. This is thought to be useful because the original costs of these assets are often the most significantly different from current values and the inclusion of the latter is considered to give information relevant to users; additionally the (corrupted) depreciation charge will restrict the income otherwise prima facie, available for dividend (subject to distribution policy).

The second corruption is the charging of the most recent production costs by using, for example, a last-in, first-out, basis of valuing inventories rather than (say) a first-in, first-out, basis; this is a practice more common in North America, for example, than in the UK. It means that in measuring income the charge for production costs is more likely to result in sufficient being held back to fund their replacement in the next cycle. In contrast, the first-in, first-out means that the earliest of the relevant costs are charged in computing income.

The Sandilands Committee examined these practices and concluded that:

> They have made present-day accounting conventions more complex and less standardised than many would consider desirable. They have strained historic cost accounting principles to breaking point.[2]

A further corruption of the pure system is the procedure of writing down asset amounts where there is doubt about its recoverability in the future; for example, the "lower of cost and net realisable value" rule used in valuing inventories. This is the prudence idea again.

If historical cost income is already misleading or difficult to understand because of the recognition and allocation judgments, how much more confusing must it be with these partial revaluations on a variety of bases?

However, for all its faults, it can provide a starting point for other systems which try to overcome the problems considered above.

References and notes

1. Companies Act 1981, Schedule 1, paragraph 12.
2. F. E. P. Sandilands, "Inflation Accounting", Report of the Inflation Accounting Committee, HMSO, 1975, page 83.

4 The General Purchasing Power Income Model

Brief history

The criticisms of the historical cost model, particularly in times of inflation, have led to the development of the purchasing power or price-level method of income measurement. During changes to general prices, comparison of capital values between two dates to measure income does not give a real measure of the change because the unit of measurement used, that is money, is changing in value and is unreliable. Essentially the purchasing power approach is based on restatement by indexation.

It was first developed comprehensively by Sweeney in the mid-1930s.[1] Since then, and particularly in the 1970s, a number of studies have been promulgated, including several by professional accounting bodies. Two such studies which achieved prominence were Provisional SSAP No 7 in the UK, which proposed indexation of historical cost amounts[2] and FAS No 33 in the USA[3] (the latter was also concerned with replacement cost accounting). Subsequently the UK Provisional Standard was withdrawn following the publication of the Sandilands Report[4] which, in the process of recommending current cost accounting (see Chapter 8), was highly critical of the method proposed by the Provisional Standard. None the less the purchasing power principle has many supporters.

Outline of approach

The procedure of indexation can be applied to any system of income measurement. Hence, it is not a "stand-alone" system. It needs as its starting point a base model; and, therefore, it follows the conventions of revenue recognition and expense matching and allocation adopted by the base model. It is most frequently applied to the historical cost model. The purpose, regardless of the base model, is to restate the values in the common denomination of stable units of purchasing power and so achieve a standard unit of measurement and a homogeneity of expression. In so doing, the effects of general inflation on the values will be eliminated. Barton uses the analogy of an elastic measuring tape which requires the purchasing power technique to compensate for the variability.[5]

The procedure is to take the base model and categorise the net assets between monetary and non-monetary; this is a fundamental distinction. Non-monetary net assets are then each restated at the beginning and end of the period in terms of common purchasing power. This is done by applying the index relevant to the date of the value of the resource; for example, if it were based on the historical cost system the relevant date would be that at which the asset was acquired. Charges for consumption, such as depreciation costs, are then based on this restated amount. Monetary assets, and liabilities, are treated differently. Because their stated value is their face value, there is no need to update the value at the end of the period; for example, if there is £1,000 in cash at the end of the period, that £1,000 remains unadjusted. The monetary assets and liabilities at the beginning of the period, however, are updated by indexation into units of purchasing power at the end of the period, and the difference between these two amounts is taken as the "gain" or "loss" arising from holding monetary assets and liabilities; usually, this "gain" or "loss" is included as income. There is much controversy about these "gains" and "losses" and this is discussed later.

Having translated the net assets into units of equivalent purchasing power – for the process is akin to that of translating from one currency to another – the revenue and expenses reported in the original income statement are translated in the same way, using either average "rates of exchange" for the period or a form of weighted average of the index if the incidence of revenue and expenses, or price changes, is particularly skewed. Depreciation charges, however, are based on the restated amount of the asset.

The result is a statement of net assets, expressed not in money but in a currency called (then) current purchasing power units. The income for the period is the revenue less the expenses, both expressed in purchasing power units, plus or minus the gain or loss on the holding of net monetary items.

Illustration

Using our example given at the Prologue and applying the translation process to the historical cost data presented in Chapter 3 gives the following outcome (all amounts presented in income statements and balance sheets in £ purchasing power units, *ie*, "£ppu's"):

		Historical cost (£)	Index factor (1)	Year 1	2	3 (before close)	3 (after close)	Total
INCOME STATEMENT								
Sales, less purchases etc (1)	Yr 1	3,000 ×	110/105	3,143				
	2	5,000 ×	121/115.5		5,238			
	3	6,000 ×	132/126.5			6,261		
Depreciation (1)	1	2,600 ×	110/100	(2,860)				
	2	2,600 ×	121/100		(3,146)			
	3	2,600 ×	132/100			(3,432)		
Gain on sale of property (2)								
Proceeds	3						11,500	
Cost	0	8,000 ×	132/100				(10,560)	
				283	2,092	2,829	940	
"Gain (loss)" on monetary items (3)								
Cash				(143)	(538)	(988)		
Bank loan				200	200	182		
Reported income (5)				340	1,754	2,023	940	5,057

		Historical cost (£)	Index factor (1)	Year 1	2	3 (before close)	3 (after close)
BALANCE SHEET	Yr						
Property (1)	1	8,000 ×	$\frac{110}{100}$	8,800			
	2	8,000 ×	$\frac{121}{100}$		9,680		
	3	8,000 ×	$\frac{132}{100}$			10,560	
Vans (1) – cost	1	7,800 ×	$\frac{110}{100}$	8,580			
	2	7,800 ×	$\frac{121}{100}$		9,438		
	3	7,800 ×	$\frac{132}{100}$			10,296	
– depn	1	2,600 ×	$\frac{110}{100}$	(2,860)			
	2	5,200 ×	$\frac{121}{100}$		(6,292)		
	3	7,800 ×	$\frac{132}{100}$			(10,296)	
				14,520	12,826	10,560	—
Cash – at face value				3,000	8,000	14,000	23,500
Total assets (5)				17,520	20,826	24,560	23,500

	Yr	Historical cost (£)	Index factor (1)	Year 1	2	3 (before close)	3 (after close)
representing –							
Capital (4)	1	13,800 ×	110/100	15,180			
	2	13,800 ×	121/100		16,698		
	3	13,800 ×	132/100			18,216	18,216
Income—							
Prior years (4)	1	340 ×	121/110		374		
	2	340 ×	132/110			408	408
	3	1,754 ×	132/121			1,913	1,913
Current year				340	1,754	2,023	2,963
				15,520	18,826	22,560	23,500
Bank loan – at face value				2,000	2,000	2,000	—
				17,520	20,826	24,560	23,500

Notes to illustration

(1) The index factor is derived by applying the index at the reporting date against the index at the point of incidence of sales and expenses, or at the date of acquisition of the asset or contribution of capital. In the case of sales and expenses, for example, the index at the end of year 1 was 110 and, with those items assumed to have accrued evenly throughout the year, the average index for the year is taken as (110 + 100) ÷ 2 = 105. For depreciation charges, non-monetary assets such as property and vans, and capital the index at the point of acquisition, in each case, was 100; thus, updating these captions to the end of year 1 means applying the index 110 against 100. Each succeeding year is updated using the same procedure.

(1)—*contd.* The adequacy or appropriateness of the index selected is a contentious issue which is discussed later.

(2) The gain on sale of property has been recalculated by updating the original cost of £8,000 to the point of sale at the end of year 3. Matching this translated amount to the proceeds received gives a surplus of £ppu 940.

(3) The controversy over the calculation of "gains" and "losses" on monetary items is discussed later. The calculations are made up thus:

	£	Index factor	"Gain (loss)" in year 1	2	3
Cash					
Beginning of year 1	—				
Arising in year 1	3,000 ×	$\frac{110-105}{105}$	(143)		
End of year 1	3,000 ×	$\frac{121-110}{110}$		(300)	
Arising in year 2	5,000 ×	$\frac{121-115.5}{115.5}$		(238)	
End of year 2	8,000 ×	$\frac{132-121}{121}$			(727)
Arising in year 3	6,000 ×	$\frac{132-126.5}{126.5}$			(261)
End of year 3 (before close)	14,000		(143)	(538)	(988)
Bank loan					
Beginning of year 1	2,000				
End of year 1	2,000 ×	$\frac{110-100}{100}$	200		
End of year 2	2,000 ×	$\frac{121-110}{110}$		200	
End of year 3 (before close)	2,000 ×	$\frac{132-121}{121}$			182
			200	200	182

The index factor used in each of the above calculations has the effect of restating the opening balance and further accounts arising during each year in the purchasing power units of the end of the year and then reducing the amounts so computed to their face value.

(4) Capital must be restated in the purchasing power units of the end of the year. Likewise income arising must be updated; thus, for example, the £ppu 340 of income in year 1 has to be re-expressed in the currency at the end of year 2 and the factor of 121/110 achieves this to give the £ppu 374 shown.

This is not the method which was explained by Provisional Standard No 7. Instead all changes to express net assets in current purchasing power units were added to opening capital. This meant that the capital became the residual amount (although the arithmetical outcome was the same as shown above). Adopting the PSSAP 7 method, for example, closing capital at the end of year 1 would be made up thus:

Opening capital		£13,800
Add	Inflation "gains" on	
	—property (£8,800 − 8,000)	800
	—vans (£8,580 − 7,800)	780
		£15,380
Less	Decline in purchasing power of bank loan – treated as income (note 3 above)	(200)
Closing capital, before inclusion of profit for year (as shown)		£15,180

(5) If a comparison or trend by year were needed it would first be necessary to translate all years' results into a common currency. Usually this would mean restating the earlier years' result in the purchasing power units of the latest year. The same point applies to any trends required of the amounts appearing in the balance sheets.

Measurement property of monetary unit

It can be seen that the measurement unit of the system is the purchasing power unit. To emphasise this point note that the property and vans are shown in £ppu's, not £s, as are the cash balances. In the latter case it happens that the face value of cash does not change and therefore that the value of cash expressed in money terms will be coincident with the value expressed in purchasing power units.

The Sandilands Committee thought that the purchasing power system, in its comprehensive application to historical cost data, was "conceptionally the most difficult method of inflation accounting suggested to us in evidence".[6] The main reason attributed to this was the use of a unit of measurement other than money. It believed that this resulted in accounting statements which were not widely understood.

Asset valuation

Assets may be expressed in the purchasing power unit, as in our example, which took the historical cost base and applied purchasing power units to it using an index. This did not give a value to the business; it could not because a translation procedure is not a valuation process. This can be demonstrated by considering the procedure which would be followed if the purchasing power approach were applied to (say) the replacement cost model. The assets would already be stated at their current (replacement) value so that these would remain unchanged; no purchasing power factor would be applied. What would change is the view of holding gains and capital, because the gains would be divided between inflationary and "real" (or relative) increases. Thus, the purchasing power approach does not help to value the capital, but it can assist in considering the amounts needed to maintain capital.

This can also be demonstrated by looking briefly at the purchasing power method advocated by Chambers which also demonstrates a simpler, one-step adjustment approach than our more commonly adopted example. Having determined the value of net assets on a current cash equivalent or realisable value basis (see Chapter 6), and having treated the changes in the value as income in accordance with the philosophy of the approach, a charge to maintain the purchasing power of shareholders' interest is then made against income and allocated to a capital maintenance reserve. The purchasing power change is measured by a general index. Thus, the valuation basis (current cash equivalent) and capital concept (purchasing power equivalent) are quite clearly separate.[7]

Concept of capital; what purchasing power?

The capital concept adopted in price-level statements is the purchasing power of the opening capital. But this begs two fundamental questions: first, "which capital?" and, second, "how should purchasing power be measured?" In our example the general purchasing power of the proprietor's capital was used because we used an index which, the data in Chapter 1 told us, was a measure of general purchasing power. In the system proposed by Provisional Standard No 7 the concept was shareholders' interest at historical cost flexed by a consumer index which was thought to reflect the consumer purchasing power of shareholders – that is, the Retail Price Index ("RPI").

In contrast the system proposed in the USA by FAS 33 recommended an index which was a reflection of general purchasing power; that is, it was not restricted to a consumer's viewpoint. Another basis is the purchasing power of the assets in which the capital has been invested.

The selection of an index is of fundamental importance. The choice depends entirely on the perception of the concept of capital. Clearly there are many choices available, but in principle they fall into the following categories:

(1) a general index relevant to the purchasing power of the proprietors or shareholders;
(2) a general index relevant to the purchasing power of the firm; and
(3) a specific index, or indices, relevant to the firm.

While a general index of shareholders' purchasing power, such as the RPI, can be said to follow the historical concept of capital with its concern for preserving shareholders' interest, use of a consumer index can be attacked on several grounds. The primary question mark over its usefulness is its relevance in that it does not try to represent the inflation suffered by a business in its day-to-day production, trading and servicing affairs. This objection relies mainly on the assumption that businesses are intent on continuity rather than liquidation, and that in this light an index which purports to measure price movements of food and consumer goods and services is irrelevant.

A second objection is that, even if the capital concept is agreed as shareholder-emphatic, it is difficult, if not impossible, to obtain an index which represents the purchasing power of all shareholders. While, for example, the RPI might approximately represent a particular band of individual shareholders in the UK, it does not represent those overseas. Additionally, it certainly does not represent the spending power of the institutional shareholders who now comprise such a large proportion of total investment in UK stock-exchange listed companies, although it might represent the individual shareholders of these institutions. The contrasting American approach with the use of a general, rather than consumer, price index might be seen as more appropriate. However, it has been argued that a general purchasing power, and a general value for money, simply do not exist[8] other than as the abstract concepts of a statistician, although the debate is by no means settled.[9]

If the generalised consumer-related indices are so heavily criticised, what of an index which relates to the purchasing power, either general or specific, of the firm? Here the capital to be maintained is that represented by the purchasing power of the firm's net assets at the beginning of the period; in short, the purchasing power of its invested capital. Hendriksen identifies three possibilities and comments on each, namely –

- Ability to re-invest in investment goods in general. This is general investment purchasing power which requires an overall investment price index. It would have the advantage of uniformity among all firms as well as ease of application.
- Ability to re-invest in capital goods purchased by all firms in the industry. This is industry investment purchasing power generally. It has the practical difficulty that many firms produce a wide variety of goods, thereby making it impossible to select the most appropriate industry index for them.
- Ability to re-invest in investment goods similar to those acquired in the past. This could represent a good approximation of the firm's specific investment purchasing power because continuity of operation over time is maintained. However, the problems of technological change can cause firms to change their investment mix. Hendriksen appears to favour this approach. It might also be used as a surrogate for specific replacement cost values using replacement cost accounting, but that is a quite separate and distinct matter which involves using the index as a valuation procedure.[10]

Even more specific to industrial firms is the measurement of purchasing power as represented by the replacement costs of the specific assets. This, of course, is similar in mechanics to replacement cost accounting (see Chapter 5), but the essential difference is that there would be no holding gains because it is purchasing power which is being measured; instead, therefore, such "gains" would be considered inflationary and would go to restate opening capital. In this context specific replacement price is not being used as a valuation process; only as a basis for the capital maintenance adjustment. But the argument all comes back to the concept of capital to be maintained. Is it the shareholders' capital or the firm's and is it a general capital or a specific one? On the view preferred will depend the index and thereby the measurement of income in £ppu's.

Classification of holding gains

The fourth key variable which was identified in Chapter 1 is the treatment of holding gains. Under price-level accounting these gains do not arise. Instead, that part of any increase in the price of an asset which has moved in line with general price increases is identified and removed from the measurement of income. It is treated as an adjustment, or restatement, of opening capital in (different) purchasing power units. We saw this clearly in our example with the sale of the property at the close of business in year 3. Of the historical cost gain of £3,500 (£11,500 − £8,000) some £ppu 2,540, representing an inflation "gain", was removed over the three years (£ppu 800 + 860 + 880) and put to capital as a restatement or price-level adjustment. Where assets are stated at some form of current value, holding gains would be split between inflationary "gains" and "real" gains. Classification of the "real" gains would then follow the philosophy of the base model.

Monetary gains and losses

There is one further feature of fundamental importance in price-level accounting and that is whether "gains" and "losses" arising upon restatement of monetary items are real and therefore should be included in the measurement of income. There is no clear agreement on what constitutes a monetary item in the first place and there are some who say that the distinction between non-monetary and monetary is arbitrary.[11] However, in addressing the main question of whether a gain or loss is encountered there seems to be merit in considering separately losses from monetary assets and gains from monetary liabilities.

There seems to be little doubt that if an individual, whose spending was typical of the consumer spending represented by the basket of goods and services in the computation of the RPI, held £1,000 in cash throughout a year when the RPI doubled, the purchasing power of the £1,000 at the end of that year would be exactly half of what it had been at the beginning. Since we have assumed that he regards cash simply as a means of procuring the goods and services represented in the RPI, he would have to borrow £1,000 at the end of the year to then have the same purchasing power as he did at the beginning. This borrowing represents a real-world event and real money; it represents a real outflow of this individual's capital. It would appear that there is indeed a loss suffered on monetary assets in this case.

This is the thrust of Lee's argument and he recommends that it would be prudent to provide against this depreciation in measuring income.[12] On the other hand, Hendriksen argues that the treatment of monetary and non monetary assets under purchasing power accounting is inconsistent. Non-monetary assets are not valued at current value but, effectively, monetary assets are; firstly, monetary assets are expressed in purchasing power units then, secondly, they are written down to their market (face) value.[13] However, even if monetary assets remained in £ppu's, the problem is only deferred and would surface when the monetary assets' (depreciated) purchasing power was utilised in the market place.

Monetary liabilities appear to be a different problem. Lee calls the "gains" which appear to arise from them "an anomaly of the book-keeping process".[14] Since it does not result in any additional cash input he excludes it from measurement of income. Another view is that it represents a reduction in the cost of the assets funded by the raising of the liability and that, accordingly, that asset cost should be adjusted. The inclusion of the gain in income would then follow the allocation process of the reduced asset cost, by depreciation or otherwise.

A further argument is that the gain is real enough but that it accrues to the owner of an entity rather than to the entity itself. A hint of this can be seen by looking at our example. It will be seen at note 4 that the movement in capital includes a charge of £ppu 200 representing the depreciation in purchasing power of the bank loan in year 1; this same £ppu 200 was added to income in accordance with the usual treatment of these items. Put another way, this amount was considered surplus to the requirement for maintenance of purchasing power and so was allocated to the proprietor as income. The bank, of course, loses the purchasing power so that the entity as a whole remains unaffected, apart from this change to the ratio of the suppliers of capital.

A final view on the subject, from the Sandilands Committee, is that in real (money) terms no gain arises from incurring a liability. Any gain must come from the use that is made of the funding which the liability represents.[15] It goes on to say that some 60% of companies replying to its survey considered that the inclusion of such gains as profit would mislead shareholders about the amount of distributable profits.[16] Further, while profitability should not be confused with distributability, it was particularly misleading to include in profit "gains" which only existed in £ppu's and not in real money terms and which, to distribute, would need cash either generated previously or from borrowings. On balance it concluded that the "gains" should be allocated direct to reserves and should not be part of income.[17]

The case for the general purchasing power income model

(1) Being a "secondary" system it assumes the benefits and problems of the primary system on which it is based; for example, if based on translation of historical cost amounts it has the advantages of that system (and most of its disadvantages) and can be claimed to be objective.
Comment The objectivity of the historical cost model has already been discussed in Chapter 3. There it was pointed out that while input data is objective the interpretation processes which are used to arrive at revenue recognition and expense allocation can be highly subjective.

(2) The process can be applied to any base model of income measurement.
Comment While true, its application to current value systems is limited to the classification of gains between "real" and inflationary; assets are not re-measured.

(3) It attempts to correct a weakness of any income system which uses a measurement unit with variable, or unstable, value. This means that price changes which represent inflationary or fictitious gains are segregated and removed from income measurement; that is, it can show how much of any gain is due to trading or holding on the one hand and to changes in monetary value on the other. Without this segregation the information is particularly misleading.

(4) Objective application is possible if independent authoritative indices are available.
Comment A particular difficulty, discussed above, is the selection of an appropriate index; preferences range from a general consumer index to a replacement cost index specific to the entity.

(5) In application the system is workable without excessive time and cost being incurred.

(6) It provides additional information to users by showing, for example, the effects of inflation on the measurement of income and the additional provisions needed to maintain the purchasing power of capital.
Comment This may be of particular use to the shareholder who is concerned for the preservation of the purchasing power of capital.

(7) In times of inflation, the price level system should provide more protection for creditors because the additional provisions made against income for the maintenance of the purchasing power of capital restrict distributions.
Comment It does not follow that, to limit distributions, income has to be charged with capital maintenance provisions. Income measurement and distribution policy are quite separate issues.

(8) The use of a stable unit of measurement should mean greater comparability of information between periods if an updating increase is first completed – for example, updating the earlier periods to restate the information in purchasing power units of the latest period. It should also aid comparability between firms.

(9) The expression of all assets is a common unit of measurement should mean that they can validly be aggregated. This is in contrast to, for example, the aggregation of assets at historical cost. As was discussed in Chapter 3, these cannot be aggregated meaningfully because they were each acquired at different times when the value of the measuring unit was different.
Comment See disadvantage (6) below.

The case against the general purchasing power income model

(1) The translation from the base model means that it continues with most of the

deficiencies of that model and its usefulness is thereby constrained; for example, consider the deficiencies of the historical cost model covered in Chapter 3.

(2) Following on (1) the realisation rule of historical cost accounting means that changes to asset prices are not recognised as they occur.

(3) Again if the historical cost base is used, the prices of all non-monetary assets are deemed to rise at the same (indexed) rate; this is false. If the specific prices have risen to higher levels than those indicated by the use of the purchasing power index, and these specific prices changes are ignored, there could be insufficient retentions for asset replacement.
Comment This, however, is more a matter of asset replacement/distribution policies rather than of the measurement of income on defined bases.

(4) Additionally interfirm comparisons can be difficult even when the same cost is incurred at the same time on different assets by two firms. When this cost is restated some time later the same amount will still appear; but if, in the intervening period, each asset's value has moved in a significantly different way, is the presentation of the same restated purchasing power useful to the user?

(5) The price level system applied to historical cost assumes that the indexed amount attributed to non-monetary assets is somehow meaningful as a storehouse of purchasing power; without knowing what the money will be spent on, this indication of purchasing power is meaningless. In any case once the money has been spent it cannot be used for other things. For example, purchasing power determined by applying consumer indices to (say) production resources does not provide useful information.

(6) Applying the translation procedure to historical cost data does not necessarily create valid additivity. Consider, for example, a company which buys a parcel of 100 shares at the beginning of the year for £1,000 and a further 100 shares in the same company at the end of the year for £1,800. If we assume that the general index adopted for price levelling moved from 100 to 120 during the year, the data would be presented like this at the year end:

	Historical cost (£s)	Index factor	Purchasing power (£ppu's)
Beginning of year – 100 shares	1,000	$\frac{120}{100}$	1,200
End of year – 100 shares	1,800	—	1,800
	2,800		3,000

The value of each parcel at the year end would be £1,800, yet different values are put on those two parcels by the price-level system.
Comment Additivity is hardly valid here in the way it would be if identical raw materials or components, purchased at different dates, were being considered.

(7) The unit of measurement, purchasing power units, is a different currency from money. The purchase power unit at the period end happens to have the same value as money at that time but the unit is an abstract concept rather than a physical unit; it therefore cannot be exchanged (see also the earlier discussion of the unit of measurement in Chapter 2).

(8) The problem over the treatment of "gains" on monetary items is unresolved and tends to cause confusion for the user because these "gains" exist only in units of purchasing power, not in money terms.

(9) The concept of a general purchasing power is questioned because, it is argued, it does not exist other than as an abstract concept; again, therefore, can purchasing power be quantified without knowing spending intentions?
Comment While this is a sound point, it is possible to overstate the argument if the price-level model is perceived as giving only a general indication of purchasing power on whatever basis is thought relevant to (a group of) users.

(10) The general purchasing power gives a measurement which is no more than indicative of the effect of price changes and which is, therefore, too broad a concept for most commercial enterprises where it has little, if any, relevance or practical use – the more so if the index is based on consumer spending. It will be noted from the earlier discussion of the problem of indices that there is no wholly suitable index for all entities.
Comment None the less, this broad indication may be of some use to shareholders, actual or potential.

(11) Care must be taken with comparisons of price adjusted data. Not only must earlier periods be updated to the latest period in a continuous process but the results then produced can still be misleading. For example, price-levelled sales figures may show a quite misleading trend if sales prices have moved in a significantly different pattern to the prices on which the index is based.

Following from these points, it might be asked whether the purchasing power approach, particularly when applied to historical cost data, provides good and relevant information for users to assist them make predictions and decisions. It appears to be considered difficult to understand and interpret, potentially misleading and to provide information not relevant to many users other than in a general way; thus, it may be thought to be not useful. For example, what does the restated information mean? The non-monetary assets are expressed at neither cost nor a reflection of market value, and capital may be translated using a generalised idea of consumer spending; the income measurement may include gains on monetary items which exist only in £ppu's.

The price-level approach may be seen as a step forward in making users aware of the effects of general increases in prices, but beyond this its usefulness is in doubt. The more that price changes related to the firm's affairs are used the greater the perceived relevance and usefulness of price-level statements. The use of the price-level technique in conjunction with some form of current value model of income measurement may be more useful to users. Current value models are considered in the two succeeding chapters.

References and notes

1. H. W. Sweeney, *Stabilized Accounting*, Harper & Row, 1936.
2. "Accounting for Changes in the Purchasing Power of Money", Provisional Statement of Standard Accounting Practice No 7, Accounting Standards Committee, 1974.

3. "Financial Reporting and Changing Prices", Statement of Financial Accounting Standard No 33, Financial Accounting Standards Board, 1979.
4. F. E. P. Sandilands, "Inflation Accounting", Report of the Inflation Accounting Committee, HMSO, 1975.
5. A. D. Barton, *The Anatomy of Accounting* (2nd edition), University of Queensland Press, 1977, page 334.
6. F. E. P. Sandilands, "Inflation Accounting", Report of the Inflation Accounting Committee, page 121.
7. R. J. Chambers, "Accounting for Inflation", Exposure Draft, University of Sydney, 1975.
8. See, for example, R. S. Gynther, "Why Use General Purchasing Power?", *Accounting and Business Research*, Spring 1974, page 141.
9. See, for example, E. O. Edwards and P. W. Bell's argument in favour of general indices of consumer spending as the best available in *The Theory and Measurement of Business Income*, University of California Press, 1961, page 278.
10. E. S. Hendriksen, *Accounting Theory* (3rd edition), Richard D. Irwin Inc, 1982, page 233.
11. *Ibid*. For example page 218. See also F. E. P. Sandilands, "Inflation Accounting", Report of the Inflation Accounting Committee, page 133.
12. T. A. Lee, *Income and Value Measurement*, Van Nostrand Reinhold (UK), 1980, page 137.
13. E. S. Hendriksen, *Accounting Theory*, page 222.
14. T. A. Lee, *Income and Value Measurement*, page 137.
15. F. E. P. Sandilands, "Inflation Accounting", Report of the Inflation Accounting Committee, page 128.
16. *Ibid*., page 120.
17. *Ibid*., page 130.

5 The Replacement Cost Income Model

Background and basis

It is sometimes argued that ideally the information needs of users are best served by the economic income measurement based on the discounted present value of anticipated future cash flows (see Chapter 7); and that, in the absence of the reasonable certainty in the data which form the inputs to that model, the practical limitations are substantial. As a rather imperfect surrogate, therefore, current market values are adopted, it being claimed that they represent a reasonable indication of the expectations of the discounted future cash flows. The replacement cost system is one of several approaches which attempts to measure income based on the current value of resources. Further, the price-level restatement system is strongly criticised because, among other reasons, it usually adopts a general index of purchasing power. Replacement cost accounting is an attempt to overcome this criticism by the use of specific prices.

The major authority for the replacement cost system is usually regarded as Edwards and Bell in a work published in 1961.[1] Others have since developed or refined the system. It should not be confused with what is sometimes referred to as current cost accounting which, while it adopts a large part of the replacement cost procedures, none the less is a system based on mixed values rather than merely replacement values. Current cost accounting is considered later in Chapter 8.

Replacement cost means the present entry value to the market or, put another way, the current sacrifice which would be incurred in the replacement of the asset. Recognition is given to absolute price changes either as they occur or, at the latest, at the next relevant accounting date; these price changes can be caused by, for example, market supply and demand, technological progress, obsolescence and general inflation. Recognition of these changes gives rise to unrealised holding gains. This is a feature of all current value systems with their attempt to focus on real-world phenomena. This overcomes a major deficiency of the transactions-based and realisations-based historical cost system. However, matching of expenses with revenue and allocations to periods can still present the kind of problems which were discussed in Chapter 2 and arbitrary treatment can arise.

The basic assumption underlying replacement cost accounting is continuity of the firm. This continuity requires that charges for the consumption of assets should be based on the cost of replacing them. Assets are viewed particularly as representing future service or operating capacity. Profit is usually measured as the difference between recognised revenues and expenses measured at their current cost. Whether such profit then represents total income depends upon the view taken of holding gains and whether these gains can be regarded as income; this is discussed later.

Illustration

We can now consider an example of the replacement cost system, using the illustrative data provided at the Prologue (all amounts in £s):

	Year				Total
	1	2	3 (before close)	3 (after close)	
INCOME STATEMENT					
Sales, less purchases etc. (1)	3,000	5,000	6,000		
Depreciation (2) –					
Year 1 9,000 ÷ 3	(3,000)				
Year 2 10,800 ÷ 3		(3,600)			
Year 3 12,000 ÷ 3			(4,000)		
Operating profit	—	1,400	2,000		
Gain on sale of property (4)			—	—	
Reported income	—	1,400	2,000	—	3,400

	Year 1	Year 2	Year 3 (before close)	Total 3 (after close)
BALANCE SHEET				
Property, at replacement cost (4)	8,900	9,900	11,500	—
Vans, at replacement cost	9,000	10,800	12,000	
depreciation charged against income (2)	(3,000)	(6,600)	(10,600)	
backlog depreciation (2) (3)		(600)	(1,400)	
Net replacement cost	6,000	3,600	—	—
Cash (5)	3,000	8,000	14,000	23,500
Total assets	17,900	21,500	25,500	23,500
representing –				
Capital				
– opening	13,800	13,800	13,800	13,800
– operating profit	—	1,400	3,400	3,400
– holding gains (2) (6)				
property,				
year 1 (8,900 − 8,000)	900	900	900	
year 2 (9,900 − 8,900)		1,000	1,000	3,500
year 3 (11,500 − 9,900)			1,600	
vans,				
year 1 (9,000 − 7,800)	1,200	1,200	1,200	
year 2 (10,800 − 9,000)		1,800	1,800	4,200
year 3 (12,000 − 10,800)			1,200	
backlog depreciation (2) (3)				
– year 2		(600)	(600)	(1,400)
– year 3			(800)	
	15,900	19,500	23,500	23,500
Bank loan (5)	2,000	2,000	2,000	—
	17,900	21,500	25,500	23,500

Notes to illustration

(1) Sales and purchases, etc., are the same as the historical cost amounts with the same basis of recognising revenue. Had Mr X held inventory there would have been a need to charge the replacement cost profit with any input price movement between the time of acquiring the inventory and its consumption in earning revenue.

(2) Holding gains and depreciation on the vans is made up thus:

		Year 1	Year 2	Year 3	Holding gains
Gross values					
Year 0 – original cost	7,800				
– holding gain	1,200				1,200
Year 1 – replacement cost	9,000	9,000			1,800
– holding gain	1,800				
Year 2 – replacement cost	10,800		10,800		
– holding gain	1,200				1,200
Year 3 – replacement cost	12,000			12,000	4,200
Depreciation charged					
Year 1 Replacement cost		(3,000)	(3,000)	(3,000)	
Year 2 Replacement cost			(3,600)	(3,600)	
Year 3 Replacement cost				(4,000)	
		6,000	4,200	1,400	
Net replacement cost should be					
Year 1 – 9,000 × 2/3		6,000			
Year 2 – 10,800 × 1/3			3,600		
Year 3 – 12,000 × 0/3				—	
Difference = backlog depreciation charged against holding gains –		—	600	1,400	
Year 2			600	600	
Year 3				800	

Strictly, depreciation charges should be based on (say) the average replacement cost for the year because this will more accurately reflect the value of the sacrifice at the point of consumption. However, using year end values is administratively convenient and usually does not result in a significant difference arising (although this depends on the timing of both the relevant price movements and the pattern of asset movements in the year). An added benefit of using year end values is that no backlog depreciation in respect of that year will arise.

(3) Backlog depreciation arises because the current year's depreciation charge only takes account of the current year's portion of the total price movement arising in the year. For example, the total price movement in the vans in year 2 was £1,800 (£10,800 − £9,000) of which ⅓ or £600 related to year 2 and was charged in the year 2 depreciation charge of £3,600 (and is the reason why the £3,000 charge of year 1 increased by £600). This left a further ⅓ or £600 relating to an expired portion of the vans' lives (year 1) which had to be charged to measure the asset properly at depreciated replacement cost. The £800 of backlog depreciation in year 3 arises from the same circumstances. Backlog depreciation has been charged against capital but there is some controversy about whether this is valid or whether it should be charged against income; this is discussed later. Note that charging it to capital means theoretically that its full replacement may not be provided for.

(4) By the time the property came to be sold its replacement cost was the same as the proceeds. (In practice there might have been some difference for expenses of sale.) Thus, all the gain on the property (£3,500) was unrealised until the end of year 3, when it became realised. The gain was recognised each year as a holding gain (see note 6).

(5) Cash is stated at face value as in the other income models using this data. The balance of £23,500 in year 3 (after close) reflects the repayment of the bank loan of £2,000 at that time.

(6) Holding gains are explained on the face of the balance sheet. In addition to the holding gains on the property (Note 4 above) there were also holding gains on the vans as indicated. Initially these are unrealised gains, but as the price movements which give rise to them are depreciated they are treated as if realised by being charged against income. For example, in year 1 the depreciation charge of £3,000 included £400 (of the holding gain of £1,200 in year 1) of "realised" holding gains; the other £800 remained unrealised. Note that the holding gains have been treated as part of capital rather than income. This is contentious and is discussed later.

(7) Given that the business closed down at the end of year 3 it might appear that the replacement basis was inappropriate. There is, after all, the underlying assumption of continuity which supports the system. However, the example is presented simply to illustrate the procedures involved in replacement cost accounting and to highlight the features.

Measurement property of monetary unit

It can be seen that the unit of measurement is money.

Asset valuation

In measuring resources on a replacement cost basis attention is focused on non-monetary assets. Monetary assets and liabilities are expressed at their face value, as are non-monetary liabilities, although these could be stated at their value to replace – and indeed should be to be conceptually consistent. An example of such non-monetary liabilities would be a provision for deferred tax if this is computed on the deferral method whereby historical rates of tax are used rather than current rates.

Non-monetary assets are usually divided into those with exchangeability and those that cannot be severed from the firm, like goodwill; the latter type are not revalued. The severable non-monetary assets – such as property, plant and equipment and inventories – are stated at their cost to replace at each accounting date – that is, at the price that would have to be paid to acquire the same type of asset. "Same type", however, can mean several things, including the same age and condition, the same service capacity or the same profit capacity. Again, technical obsolescence can mean there is no price available for the existing asset. One method of overcoming this is to use the price of a newer, more sophisticated, model and adjust for the additional capacity or profit potential inherent in this model. Depreciating assets are valued at a written down cost to replace. Usually this means valuing the asset at its replacement cost new and then adjusting this value for the number of years' service already given. This gives rise to backlog depreciation, as our example demonstrated, and this is discussed later.

Replacement cost is usually estimated by direct pricing from suppliers or from specific asset or industry indices as a surrogate for direct pricing. As Lee points out, however, determination of appropriate prices may not always be easy. There may not be a ready or a representative market. He identifies three conditions which should be met in the evaluation process:

(1) the values should be objective commercial values, not imaginary ones;
(2) the values should be based on "normal" quantities for the entity rather than exceptional bulk purchasing; and
(3) the markets from which the values are derived, ideally, should be free, active and representative.[2]

If specific indices are used this will give an asset measurement identical to the amount derived in the price-level accounting system were that same index used there also. There are, however, two important differences. In the price-level system, as indicated earlier, the process was one of restatement not of asset measurement; conversely, with replacement cost accounting, use of the index gives an asset measurement. The second distinction is that the "gain" arising from the use of the specific index is treated as an inflationary gain under price-level accounting – that is, as a restatement of opening capital; in using replacement cost accounting it will be classified as a holding gain. As will be discussed shortly, holding gains might be treated as either capital maintenance (that is, a restatement of opening capital) or income.

Concept of capital

The concept of capital is usually perceived as the aggregate productive capacity of the firm's assets including, in some applications, net monetary assets used in the earnings process; this is concerned with the capital of the entity rather than of the shareholders or proprietors. Capital is viewed as part of operating capacity which must be maintained before income can be said to have been earned. Operating capacity is usually taken to mean ability to produce a given volume of goods, so maintaining the physical level of operations and preserving the firm as a going concern. As Barton points out, however, maintenance of a physical level of operation, by setting aside enough for the replacement of assets, does not necessarily imply that the assets actually will be replaced. Indeed no further action is implied. This is because the measurement process merely adopts the maintenance of operating capacity as a benchmark for income measurement which is considered useful to users. But such a process is not concerned with specific ends. The decision to replace or not is an investment decision, as indeed is the decision to maintain a given operating capacity.[3]

A further aspect of operating capacity maintenance was touched on when considering price-level accounting. This related to the division of absolute, or specific, price increases into their constituents of inflationary "gain" and "real" gain. If we consider our example again we can see that holding gains in year 1 amounted to £2,100 (being £900 for property and £1,200 for vans). However, the general price index moved from 100 to 110 in year 1 (see Prologue) so that these holding gains might be analysed thus:

Inflationary "gains"	
Property – $£8{,}000 \times \frac{110-100}{100}$	£800
Vans – $£7{,}800 \times \frac{110-100}{100}$	780
	£1,580
Total gains	2,100
"Real" or relative gains	£520

This analysis may not really matter if holding gains are not regarded as income because they are all then restatements of capital. Indeed the Sandilands Committee described the distinction as "meaningless", arguing that it was based on the implicit, and in its view false, assumption that the price increases suffered by a company were due in part to inflation measured by a general index which had no relevance to a company's spending habits.[4]

However, if holding gains are regarded as income, the above analysis might indicate that only £520 should be included, with the remaining £1,580 being a "fictitious" gain representing a restatement of opening capital and allocated accordingly.

Classification of holding gains

The question of which holding gains (both realised and unrealised) should be regarded as income was covered briefly in Chapter 2 and there it was stated that their classification depended entirely on the perception of the concept of capital. If capital is regarded as the productive capacity of assets, then any change in the market (entry) prices of these assets represents a capital maintenance adjustment. Put another way, the surplus arising from the increase in market prices could not be distributed as income because the productive capacity has not increased and such a distribution would reduce, or impair, the command over this stock of productive capacity. The gains represent mere fluctuations in the prices of the assets representing the capital base of capacity but do not add to this capital base. In short, they do not show an increase in capital under this concept; therefore they cannot be regarded as income.

This can be illustrated by returning to our example. If we assume that Mr X wished to continue the business into year 4 and beyond, the realised holding gain on the property (£3,500) would be required as part of the capital needed to replace the one sold. Distributing it as income in these circumstances would impair the capital of the entity. The effect of following this concept of capital is that holding gains are not included in the statement of income unless they relate to assets which were, or are, surplus to operating requirements and so form no part of productive capacity.

Adopting a concept of capital does not necessarily mean that the capital need remain fixed in terms of that concept. For example, a reduction in the need for productive capacity will mean a release of capital to income just as expansion of it will mean greater demands on income. As was mentioned in Chapter 2, in discussing distribution policy, the expansion and contraction of capacity was addressed particularly by the UK Exposure Draft No 18, published in 1976, which suggested an appropriation account into which would go operating profit and out of which would come dividends to shareholders; it was also the "marshalling yard" for directors to consider future capital needs in the light of contraction/expansion.[5] This is a useful illustration of the clear distinction which must be drawn between income measurement and distribution policy. The appropriation account idea was abhorred by some because of its lack of "objectivity"; that is, directors could exercise judgment and it was difficult to "verify" this judgment.

A contrary view of the concept of capital is that it is the money value of a stock of assets. Increases in this value represent increases to wealth which are, therefore, income; such increments can be distributed without impairing the money value of the capital.

The debate about classification of holding gains can be overstressed. Holding gains, on either concept, give an indication of an important part of a firm's commercial activities, namely, the quality of its buying performance (generally the higher the gain the better the performance); so the amount of holding gains, regardless of their classification as capital or income, should be interpreted alongside the performance indicated by the operating profit. In two otherwise identical companies, for example, the one with the higher holding gains can be looked on more favourably.

Holding "gains" can be seen as savings on the cost of the related asset; thus, with the operating capacity concept of capital, they represent the additional cost burden which will have to be provided for purchase of the replacement asset.

A refinement of the holdings gains debate is the treatment of backlog depreciation. In our example above it was seen how this can arise (see notes to illustrations 2 and 3). The controversy is over where this depreciation should be charged – against income or capital? If holding gains are already considered as income the solution is straightforward – the backlog depreciation, also being a (realised) holding gain, should be charged against income.

In most replacement cost models, however, holding gains are considered as capital because the model follows the operating capacity concept of capital. Here the answer is not so clear. Charging backlog depreciation to capital means that full provision for its replacement will not have been made by the time replacement is due. The deficiency of provision will be the aggregate backlog depreciation and only charging it against income will make good this deficiency. Arguments against doing this centre on the corruption of the income measurement by the introduction of an extra-period charge. This charge, it is argued, has nothing to do with the proportion of the asset consumed in the revenue-generating process for the year; and this is what the depreciation allocation against income is supposed to represent. Instead, charging it against income would change the nature of the depreciation charge to a part-provision for replacement.

The problem may be more apparent than real. Backlog depreciation arises because there is a time-lag in actually investing, in a replacement asset, the funds charged as the value consumed; these charges will only provide for replacement if the asset is replaced immediately. During this time-lag the price increases further, leaving the amount charged inadequate for replacement. However, in a company with several long-term assets there may still be this re-investment time-lag on each separate asset, but old assets are being replaced with new – usually on a regular basis. Thus, in terms of aggregate re-investment in replacement there is no time-lag. In other words, replacement expenditure is at least as much as aggregate depreciation charges. It is argued that "robbing Peter to pay Paul" in this way reduces the importance of the debate about backlog depreciation and may eliminate it. Indeed, so long as the funds which represent the depreciation are invested otherwise than in cash – that is, in assets which either earn income or appreciate in value – the value of the backlog depreciation provision should be maintained, thereby setting aside sufficient for replacement.

By eliminating holding gains from income, if the productive capacity concept is adopted, and by recognising price changes as they arise rather than as they are realised by a transaction, replacement cost income represents operating income – that is, an increase in quantities or volume as discussed in Chapter 2.[6] This emphasis on activities rather than on transactions means that the current period's income measurement reflects the economic events of the period. Unlike income measured by historical cost accounting, or by figures translated from such data and expressed in purchasing power units, the income for the period is not so likely to include income relating to prior periods (whose recognition has been deferred until realisation).

Monetary gains and losses

One further feature needs comment. The income model excludes any of the "gains" and "losses" on monetary items which cause so much controversy in price-level accounting. Replacement cost accounting is sometimes criticised for this exclusion. There are two points which can be made in reply. Firstly, given that the unit of measurement is money, a monetary liability can only be expressed at face value in money terms; the "gain" arises only when there is translation to purchasing power units. Secondly, as indicated earlier, the gain arises not so much from incurring the liability over a period of inflation but in the investment in assets funded by the liability. Any gain arising is not explicitly shown and accrues to the shareholders of the entity at the expense of the loan creditor; the income of the entity is unaffected.

This can be demonstrated by looking at our example again. In year 1 holding gains on the property and vans were all allocated to the shareholders, although the bank funded some £2,000 towards purchase of property one year previously; a comparison of the capital and liabilities appearing in the balance sheets at the beginning and end of year 1 shows the following (income can be ignored but, in any case, was nil in year 1):

	Opening	%	Closing	%
Capital	£13,800	87	£15,900	89
Bank loan	2,000	13	2,000	11
	£15,800	100	£17,900	100

Thus, the capital supplier's ratio has changed. The proprietor's interest in the business has grown from 87% to 89% and the bank's interest has declined accordingly – and all due to the allocation of holding gains, in their entirety, to the proprietor.

The case for the replacement cost income model

(1) The realisation rule central to historical cost accounting is jettisoned and, with it, much of the conservatism concept. Thus, a transactions-based system gives way to one which reflects the activities and events of the period. Points (2) to (6) below indicate consequences of this change which are considered beneficial.

(2) Price changes are recognised as they occur and, adopting the operating capacity capital concept, the resultant holding gains are eliminated from the measurement of income. This measure, therefore, reflects the result of operating during the period.
Comment As indicated earlier, it is also useful to review a firm's buying performance as evidenced by its holding gains.

(3) The measurement of periodic income tends to be undistorted by income relating to prior periods. Contrast this to the historical cost system, for example, where recognition of income is deferred until realisation, which means that any measure of historical cost periodic income is a hotch-potch of current and prior years and of unidentified and unquantified holding gains (see point (4) below). Thus, the potentially misleading trends of the widely used historical cost model are avoided as is the problem of interperiod and interfirm comparisons.
Comment The elimination of holding gains from measured income under replacement cost models may be misleading if it causes attention to be focused exclusively on reported operating income. Many entities depend to a significant degree on, for example, their efficient purchasing of inventories at economic prices rather than on productive efficiency. Yet it is only the result of the latter which is included in the income measurement. Buying performance, as indicated by the extent of holding gains, should also be considered.

(4) Holding gains, their source and amount, are identified (in contrast to the historical cost system).

(5) Recognition of price changes as they occur means that the possibilities for "income-smoothing" at the discretion of management are reduced. The timing of those transactions which trigger price change recognition is no longer relevant.

(6) The segregation of holding gains from operating income should contribute to more accurate budgeting because each is usually dependent on different factors.

(7) Income is measured in money terms which are current. Further, the unit of measurement is money which is easy to understand (in contrast to the difficulties with the purchasing power unit).

(8) The balance sheet represents a statement of current values of resources. Thus, interfirm comparison is helped.
Comment This also remedies a popular misunderstanding of what the historical cost balance sheet represents. But the current values shown by the replacement cost model assume continuity of the entity. While this is relevant to some users, there will be others to whom another base is more useful.

(9) The determination of income by reference to activities and events and the measurement of assets by reference to current (replacement) values mean that a meaningful rate of return on capital employed can be calculated.
Comment It could also be appropriate to include consideration of holding gains against capital employed.

(10) The operating capacity of the firm, however this capacity is measured, is preserved by the charge against income for the current replacement cost of assets consumed in the revenue-generating activities.

(11) By focusing attention on operating profit and by segregating holding gains it assists in financing and dividend policies.

Comment This does not imply any particular asset replacement or distribution policies. These, as was indicated earlier, are separate issues.

(12) The replacement cost system tends to promote efficiency by focusing attention on the need to review product selling prices regularly and to review production policies and methods as input costs change.
Comment It is possible to overstate this argument. The well-managed entity will regularly review selling prices and production methods.

(13) There is a strong and relevant emphasis on the continuity of the firm by concentration on the replacement of assets, preservation of operating capacity and elimination of holding gains from operating profit.

(14) The retention of the historical cost transactions base means that, with some experience, the replacement cost system is neither difficult nor costly to implement. Further, historical cost income can be measured, if wished, from the replacement cost operating profit by deducting unrealised holding gains and adding realised holding gains from previous periods.

(15) All these points culminate, it is claimed, in a measure of income and a statement of current values which reflect real world phenomena, which are relevant and which, therefore, provide useful information to users for decision making.
Comment This is an ambitious claim which does not altogether stand up. For some purposes of some users these claims are no doubt valid; for other users, for example those interested in a realisation value of the entity, clearly the information is of limited value.

The case against the replacement cost income model

(1) Much of the data used is based on conventions which are open to attack (as they were in the historical cost model); for example, the recognition of operating revenue retains a conservative approach on realisation, and expenses allocations on depreciation continue to be arbitrary.

(2) The measurement of income is lost in a series of significant and subjective value judgments on replacement costs which reduces the "objectivity" and "factual" base of the information needed for stewardship reporting. There are occasions when the estimate of replacement cost is so esoteric and remote from real-world phenomena that its usefulness is questioned. (See also point (7) below.)

(3) Intangible resources are not evaluated. These represent sources of real value to an entity, even if they are usually not separately exchangeable. Thus, if replacement cost income is meant as a surrogate for economic income it does not, and cannot, succeed because intangibles can be a source of significant cash flow.
Comment This criticism is not unique to the replacement cost model. All models considered in this text, other than the economic income model, ignore the systematic evaluation of intangibles. Even when such intangibles do appear, as in the historical cost model, they only appear because a transaction has created a need to account for the cost; their appearance does not then indicate replacement or realisable value.

(4) Replacement cost accounting does not appear to be suitable for all entities – for example, value-based companies such as insurance companies and commodity dealers whose profit from operating could be classified as holding gains.
Comment It might be reasonable for such entities to include holding gains in operating profit in most circumstances.

(5) While the replacement cost of assets provides a useful measure in most cases, there are instances where realisable value or economic value are more useful, such as when the

capacity represented by the asset will not be replaced but sold; such instances are ignored and this makes the replacement cost income measurement too rigid.
Comment This is part of the argument in favour of the mixed values approach considered later in Chapter 8.

(6) "Gains" and "losses" on monetary items are not reflected in replacement cost income. (This argument was discussed earlier.)

(7) There are many practical difficulties in determining the appropriate costs to replace; to overcome these can be costly in time and money. The exercise can involve profound questions of policy (which change from time to time) as well as problems with technological progress, modern equivalent capacity, substitute capacity and obsolescence. As well as this, actually finding sources of suitable replacement cost information can sometimes be very difficult, especially in specialised industries.
Comment There is no doubt that practical difficulties can be significant. The report of the CCA Monitoring Working Party in the UK indicated areas of practical difficulty encountered by industrial and commercial companies in many different industries, particularly when attempting to arrive at a replacement cost for property, plant and equipment.[7] Consider, for example, the problems in determining an appropriate replacement cost for a computer of a given capacity or the modern computerised equivalent of a telephone switchboard; or the value to be attributed to the dry dock of a declining ship repairer.

(8) The accuracy of much of the replacement cost measures, if specific indices are being used, will depend on the adequacy of the supporting historical cost records, particularly for property plant and equipment and inventories. If these records are inadequate for this purpose the replacement cost measure could be misleading.

(9) The effects of general inflation are ignored (unless specific steps are taken to account for them). Thus, absolute price changes are not analysed between those which are due to inflation and those which are "real".

(10) In times of falling prices the allocation of holding losses against capital will mean a higher operating profit than is shown by the historical cost measurement.
Comment This assumes that the historical cost model is somehow "better". In these circumstances it is merely more cautious.

(11) Comparison of results over time is difficult because of the need to update each year by some form of purchasing power.
Comment To meet this criticism the use of a generalised index – for example, in the UK the consumer Retail Price Index – has been suggested by some.

The replacement cost system is thought by many to answer many of the problems of historical cost and purchasing power methods of income measurement and, therefore, to represent a substantial improvement. There are, however, difficulties in applying it universally and rigidly to all entities in all circumstances. These difficulties, both theoretical and practical, have given rise to a related approach which considers mixed values as a more useful basis for users. This is considered later in Chapter 8.

References and notes

1. E. O. Edwards and P. W. Bell, *The Theory and Measurement of Business Income*, University of California Press, 1961.
2. T. A. Lee, *Income and Value Measurement*, Van Nostrand Reinhold (UK), 1980, page 72.
3. A. D. Barton, *The Anatomy of Accounting*, University of Queensland Press, 1977, page 361.
4. F. E. P. Sandilands, "Inflation Accounting", Report of the Inflation Accounting Committee, HMSO, page 148.
5. "Current Cost Accounting", Exposure Draft No 18, Accounting Standards Committee, 1976. This Exposure Draft was prepared as the flesh on the skeleton of the Sandilands Report (qv).
6. In effect, removing holding gains from the income measurement is the same as using the same prices at both the opening and closing dates of the period. Increase in value remaining after this, therefore, must relate to increases in volume.
7. "Report of the CCA Monitoring Working Party", Accounting Standards Committee, 1983.

6 The Current Cash Equivalent Income Model

Background and basis

The second of the two current value systems of income measurement is based on the market realisable values of resources. It is sometimes known as the current cash equivalent or continuously contemporary accounting ("COCOA"). The principal current proponent of this approach for the last thirty years is generally recognised as Chambers,[1] although MacNeal is accredited as the originator in the 1930s.[2]

Stocks of resources are regarded as having relevance to decisions about the future ony if they can be converted by exchange into other resources. This means that assets must be exchangeable – that is, have severability. This is why Chambers' definition of an asset includes exchangeability as a prime condition (see earlier discussion in Chapter 2). Given this severability, the most relevant information about resources in looking to the future, it is argued, is market selling price because this gives freedom of choice or adaptability:

> Many of us say that the value of an object to its owner is its cost (meaning its price); which is patently false, for otherwise the owner would surely have preferred to have the money which gives him greater freedom of choice.[3]

Few intangibles would be included in the balance sheets other than (say) patents; again specialised plant and equipment would tend to have a relatively low market selling value soon after purchase (perhaps even zero).

The interpretation of the going concern concept is quite different from that adopted for the replacement cost model, where the emphasis was on continuity of the same or similar activities. Going concern and replacement of resources with the current cash equivalent basis is interpreted as the ability to adapt to circumstances by the sale of assets in the ordinary course of business. Capital is regarded as a cash fund available for any use and represents, therefore, a form of generalised purchasing power although expressed in units of money, not of purchasing power. While valued by reference to current cash equivalent, a one-step price-level adjustment has also been suggested by Chambers to preserve the purchasing power of opening capital in terms of general inflation.[4]

The basis of the approach is opportunity or alternative cost; that is, value is determined by measuring what is being sacrificed by having the resources in their present form as opposed to the most attractive alternative. This alternative is the higher of realisable value of the resources in their present form or the present discounted value of future cash flows to be generated from investing the realised proceeds. Because of the impracticalities of estimating the latter with any degree of certainty, realisable value is usually taken as the opportunity cost.

Clearly determination of selling values will not always be straightforward. Some of the more problematical circumstances are referred to later. With property, plant and equipment, increases to the selling price between the beginning and end of the period are regarded as gains. Falls in selling value are regarded as the charge for depreciation in lieu of the more formalised allocation procedures of other income models; this aims to relate the charge to the physical depreciation of the assets by wear and tear and obsolescence.

The measurement of income is clearly seen as the difference between the amount of wealth at two dates. The realisation concept is abandoned. All non-monetary assets are revalued at selling price on acquisition and at all subsequent accounting dates until disposal. Thus, price changes, or holding gains and losses, are recognised at the point of acquisition rather than at disposal. This makes the former point critical in the operating cycle in contrast to the other models reviewed so far, all of which regarded sales recognition as the trigger point. Subsequent actual realisation merely exchanges one asset for another of more generalised purchasing flexibility as well as confirming or "fine-tuning" the original estimate.

There are implications for the prudence concept. On the one hand, with no realisation concept, the recognition of revenue is less cautious; on the other hand, with the emphasis on the realisability and severability of assets, resources which do not meet these criteria are evaluated at nil value. Thus, as indicated above, intangibles such as goodwill and deferred start-up costs are not recognised. It can be also seen that matching of costs to recognised revenues is not an issue.

Illustration

We can now consider an example of continuously contemporary accounting using the illustration data from the Prologue (all amounts in £s):

	Year 1	Year 2	Year 3 (before close)	Year 3 (after close)	Total
INCOME STATEMENT					
Purchases and other expenses (1)	9,000	14,000	17,000		
Gains from operating/ holding (1)	3,000	5,000	6,000		
Depreciation (2)	(2,000)	(2,800)	(3,000)		
Gain on property (3)	800	900	1,800		
	1,800	3,100	4,800		
Capital maintenance (5)	(1,380)	(1,560)	(1,700)		
Reported income	420	1,540	3,100		5,060
BALANCE SHEET					
Property (4)	8,800	9,700	11,500	—	
Vans (4)	5,800	3,000	—	—	
	14,600	12,700	11,500	—	
Cash	3,000	8,000	14,000	23,500	
Total assets	17,600	20,700	25,500	23,500	
representing –					
Capital – opening	13,800	13,800	13,800	13,800	
– maintenance (5)	1,380	2,940	4,640	4,640	
– income (5) (6)	420	1,960	5,060	5,060	
	15,600	18,700	23,500	23,500	
Bank loan	2,000	2,000	2,000	—	
	17,600	20,700	25,500	23,500	

Notes to illustration

(1) Purchases are presented this way simply to demonstrate that this is the key factor and that the gains are regarded as having arisen from this activity.

(2) Depreciation is calculated as the difference between the realisable value of the vans at the beginning and end of each year:

	Year 1	Year 2	Year 3	Total
Cost	7,800			
Estimated realisable value				
– beginning of year	N/A	5,800	3,000	
– end of year	(5,800)	(3,000)	—	
Proceeds (scrapped)	—	—	—	
Depreciation	2,000	2,800	3,000	7,800

Note that the aggregate depreciation charged against income is the original historical cost (£7,800).

(3) Property gains are recognised each year. Selling values are below the cost to replace. In essence the difference relates to the estimated expenses of selling. The calculations are:

	Year 1	Year 2	Year 3
Cost	(8,000)		
Estimated realisable value			
– beginning of year	N/A	(8,800)	(9,700)
– end of year	8,800	9,700	11,500
Gain	800	900	1,800

The proceeds of sale of £11,500 are not dealt with in the income statement because all gains have already been recognised in unrealised form.

(4) Property and vans are expressed at estimated realisable value.

(5) The capital maintenance reserve is computed as a one-step price-level adjustment to preserve the purchasing power of opening capital and retained income by reference to general price changes. Despite the basis of the calculations this is expressed in money and not purchasing power units. Details are as follows:

	Year 1	Year 2	Year 3
Opening capital	13,800	13,800	13,800
Capital maintenance adjustment (see below)			
Year 1	1,380	1,380	1,380
Year 2		1,560	1,560
Year 3			1,700
		2,940	4,640
Retained income			
Year 1	420	420	420
Year 2		1,540	1,540
Year 3			3,100
		1,960	5,060
	15,600	18,700	23,500
Index factor	$\frac{110-100}{100}$	$\frac{121-110}{110}$	$\frac{132-121}{121}$
Multiplied by	×	×	×
Opening capital	13,800		
Opening capital, opening maintenance adjustment and opening retained income		15,600	18,700
Capital maintenance adjustment =	1,380	1,560	1,700

(6) Income covers all gains, both operating and holding.

Measurement property of monetary unit

From this example and the earlier discussion the unit of measurement is clearly money rather than any form of purchasing power units.

Asset valuation

Assets are measured at current realisable value or opportunity cost but, as stressed earlier, the assets must possess the quality of exchangeability so as to be able to add to the stock of cash or purchasing power. The selling price to be adopted is that which would be realised in an orderly disposal rather than in a forced sale such as a liquidation. Where assets are only part-complete, as with work in progress inventories, the selling values should be those at the time of valuation rather than (say) future sales values for the completed products less estimated costs to complete. This approach stresses the underlying theme of assessing the adaptability of the enterprise and its generalised purchasing power. It can lead to zero values for some part-complete inventories and raw materials because usually there is little, if any, market for such goods. This is even more likely if the goods are perishable. The availability of selling values for property and for plant and equipment will tend to vary according to how generalised or specialised are the assets. As indicated earlier very specialised assets may have no market selling value or perhaps even a negative value if there are expenses of disposal. Consequently, depreciation charges of specialised assets are likely to be relatively high in the first years of use. These procedures, however, might be modified by the use of surrogates for selling price such as replacement costs and of more subjective computations of depreciation charges. It can be seen that, for example, a manufacturing company may have little selling value in its assets relative to purchase cost – the more so if it is a particularly specialised activity and situated in a geographically remote area.

Concept of capital

The concept of capital is the purchasing power or cash equivalent of the shareholders' equity. Income is earned, therefore, only after this generalised purchasing power over goods and services has been maintained, including the one-step price-level charge for the maintenance of purchasing power in terms of general inflation. As indicated earlier, while the capital concept relates to purchasing power, it is expressed in money terms. This is demonstrated by referring to our example and to note 5 in particular.

It can be seen that the capital maintenance adjustment, based on the movement in general prices in each year, has been made to preserve opening capital purchasing power but that the income remaining after this adjustment is expressed in money terms both for the year and all years aggregated. If each year's income, however, were restated to the next year's index level, the amount then appearing would be expressed in £ppu's and not £s.

This concept of capital means that any increase in generalised purchasing power is income because it means there are more proceeds potentially available from realisation than hitherto; that is, this surplus can be consumed without impairing the command over goods and services which existed at the beginning.

This can be contrasted to the need of the replacement cost model to maintain a physical operating base.

Classification of holding gains

All holding gains are regarded as income. But their recognition at the acquisition point and the use of selling prices makes it difficult to segregate them from operating income. This, however, can be a meaningless distinction here in any case. For example, if a retailer bought a product for £7 and it had a realisable value of £10 is the £3 difference, which is recognised on purchase, a holding gain or an operating profit?

The adoption of the acquisition point as the key factor in the operating cycle has implications for the timing of the recognition of gains. For those assets in a condition for sale in the normal course of trade, such as an inventory of finished goods, this recognition will generally be earlier than with the replacement cost model. Conversely, for those assets which are not in a condition for sale in the ordinary course of business, such as work in progress or plant and equipment, the current cash equivalent model will tend to value them at lower realisation prices than costs to replace. Thus, assuming rising prices, in the complete cycle from cash to investment to sale/disposal to cash, holding gains on most assets will be recognised earlier and to a greater extent with the replacement cost model than with the current cash equivalent approach; as realisation approaches, the current cash equivalent model will catch up by recognising the gains which now start to accrue. In essence the distinction is about the difference between entry (input) values and exit (output) values on a period by period basis. Replacement cost accounting generally has a more accelerated pattern of recognition of holding gains although, as discussed in Chapter 5, they are not necessarily treated as income.

The inclusion of holding gains in income is similar in principle to the economic income model (see Chapter 7), which does not distinguish between holding and operating gains. The essential distinction is the capital concept. With continuously contemporary accounting this is related to shareholders' interests in contrast to the economic income model which is concerned to preserve the value of resources consumed in the period.

The case for the current cash equivalent income model

(1) By taking account of the alternative uses to which an entity's resources may be put, the adaptability of the enterprise can be assessed. This is particularly important where the market in which the firm operates is volatile and the future is especially uncertain. A high value of assets relative to cost, such as in a property dealing company, will indicate good adaptability. The property company can move in and out of the market (and other markets) fairly readily. Conversely a low value relative to replacement costs, such as with a highly specialised capital intensive industry like an oil refinery, will show low adaptability. Likewise the degree of adaptability indicates the risk in the investment. For example, the lower the ratio of current cash equivalent value to replacement cost of long-term assets, the more confident the investor must be about the returns over the years.
Comment The above example is a good illustration of how one income model can assist another and how no single income theory is universally versatile.

(2) Because assets are measured at their opportunity cost – that is, the sacrifice made by holding the asset rather than selling it, comparison of the relative merits of continuing to use assets and, alternatively, selling them is made easy. This can be done on an individual asset basis or with a group of assets. It can also be done for the entire firm. Proponents would argue that this is particularly relevant data and therefore useful.

(3) The emphasis on cash funds and generalised purchasing power makes the information useful to those with an interest in the shorter term of the firm. For example, creditors may be less concerned about future profitability and the chances of the firm surviving in the medium to long term; estimates of future income streams are less relevant to such creditors in these circumstances. The current cash equivalent data enables an assessment of existing asset cover.

(4) The data provided is more comparable among firms. The use of exit values with the emphasis on generalised purchasing power, achieves this. In contrast the replacement cost model shows entry values to the particular firm only and so comparability is more limited.
Comment While true comparability among several firms can be overstated, especially where those firms are in quite different industries, within the same industry replacement costs can also provide reasonable comparison (see also point 8 below on the "case against").

(5) Selling prices are easy to understand and they achieve a statement of worth in the balance sheet in a way which other systems do not; for example, the historical cost system provides a list of residual unallocated original costs, while the replacement cost model shows entry values corrupted by income and expense recognition and allocation procedures which make the information more difficult to understand.
Comment Although the model is easier to understand, this does not mean that it is somehow a "better" measure of worth. The appropriateness of the measurement theory is dependent on the uses for which intended (see also point 8 below on the "case against").

(6) The system is the logical extension of what is practised already in the historical cost system; as examples, consider the rule of expressing inventory value at the lower of original cost and net realisable value and the disclosure of market values for investments.
Comment In the historical cost system such realisability rules have their source in the prudence concept and are adopted because the costs are unlikely to be recovered through use or sale. But the emphasis for longer term resources is on use rather than sale, and to claim that the current cash equivalent approach is a logical extension may be to stretch the point beyond credence.

The case against the current cash equivalent income model

(1) The system emphasises the short term when, in fact, most firms operate for the medium to long term. This, in essence, is the difference in interpretation of the going concern concept between continuity on the one hand and adaptability on the other. The assumption of the current cash equivalent model is that assets are regarded as a means of meeting obligations to creditors. In most cases this is false, repayment of creditors coming from future operations and the net cash inflows generated. For most managements, therefore, the information provided is not relevant and certainly not as relevant and useful as that provided by the replacement cost system with its emphasis on continuity and the future (and hence on future prospects). This, it is argued, is a more realistic view to take than that indicated by the current realisable value model, which is too simplistic in approach. Adaptability becomes relevant only if the firm is in financial difficulty; otherwise the assumption of realisation of resources is questionable.
Comment None the less, for creditors the indication of realisable resources may be useful.

(2) The emphasis on the short term rather than on the medium to long term also shows in the failure to provide for the replacement of assets. As our example demonstrated, depreciation charged aggregates the original historical cost of assets. There is, therefore, the same problem as was encountered with the historical cost system in that provisions for replacement of assets is not considered necessary before the income is determined. There is the real danger of contraction of the business if asset replacement is not provided for.
Comment The question of asset replacement policy (and also distribution policy) has been discussed in earlier chapters. Such replacement is an issue which is quite separate from that of income measurement, as is distribution policy.

(3) Recognising income at the point of acquisition of assets, such as inventories, rather than at some subsequent point closer to sale is less than cautious when the sale at the assumed selling price is not assured. Thus, there could be a build-up of inventories with profit taken on acquisition; this profit would be distributable. If sale at this profit is not subsequently achieved there could be significant financial difficulty.
Comment As indicated above, distribution policy is a separate issue from income measurement. The earning of income is not, of itself, sufficient to justify its distribution. Many other factors need to be considered, such as liquidity, effect on gearing (or leverage) through borrowing to enable distribution, expansion/contraction of activities and the need to replace assets.

(4) Firms engaged in highly specialised activities have their income measurement distorted in years when significant re-equipping takes place. Such expenditure effectively is charged against income as depreciation in the year of purchase because it has little, if any, realisable value. Subsequent years' income is likewise distorted by very low charges for depreciation. To managements concerned about future operations – and clearly such concern is real if there has been investment in new equipment – such distortion results in an irrelevant income measurement.

(5) The same point applies also to those firms with significant resources which are not exchangeable. Thus, for example, a computer company engaged in developing advanced software would perhaps find that much research and development expenditure would not be recognised as an asset because it is not exchangeable and has to be charged against income as incurred, thereby creating an arguable mismatching of expenses with subsequent eventual revenue.

(6) Following on points (2), (3), (4) and (5) above it can be seen that a specialist manufacturing company which is growing quickly and which therefore has significant outlays

on plant, equipment and inventories, and which also is developing new products will report a current cash equivalent income figure which is of little relevance to the very rationale behind the growth – namely, the future. And likewise, in subsequent years of stability, income will be measured without first matching the expenditure which helped to generate it.

(7) The determination of current selling prices is difficult because there is often no ready market. This, in many cases, results in values which are more akin to liquidation values, with consequent implications for the usefulness of the income measurement derived. Additionally, the values adopted can be highly subjective.

(8) Given the difficulties of determining selling values, surrogates are sometimes suggested in their place. Thus, income can be determined by a mixture of several valuation bases which makes the measurement confusing and difficult to understand. Again, aggregation of these different values in the balance sheet is acceptable only if the surrogates are valid; otherwise there cannot be additivity.

The current cash equivalent system, with the additional one-step price-level adjustment of shareholders' equity, is a hybrid system combining the realisable value basis of asset measurement with a purchasing power concept of capital. Even without the price-level adjustment, the capital is still viewed as a measure of the command over goods and services in general.

Of the two main current value models of income measurement there is little to choose between them when replacement costs of assets and realisable values are very similar. When they are significantly different, however, the current cash equivalent system is useful for some purposes either related to the short term or to the adaptability of the firm; in contrast, replacement cost accounting is useful in looking to continuity in the future along similar lines to the past. Essentially, then, the two current value systems respond to different demands and can be said to be complementary rather than competing.

References and notes

1. R. J. Chambers, *Accounting, Evaluation, and Economic Behaviour*, Prentice-Hall, 1966.
2. R. MacNeal, *Truth in Accounting*, University of Pennsylvania Press, 1929 (re-printed by Scholars Book Co, 1970).
3. R. J. Chambers, "Prospective Adventures in Accounting Ideas", *The Accounting Review*, April 1967; re-printed in *Accounting Finance and Management*, Butterworths, 1969, page 687.
4. R. J. Chambers, "Accounting for Inflation", Exposure Draft, University of Sydney, 1975.

7 The Economic Income Model

Background and basis

The concept of economic income is closely associated with the economist's view of personal income transposed into a business environment. It is linked clearly to the maintenance of "welloffness" as discussed in Chapter 2, with welloffness or capital being viewed as the discounted value of future anticipated cash flows of the firm, using the discounting rate considered appropriate. Periodic income using this approach can be said to be the difference between the values of opening and closing capital of a period.

In discussing the valuation of capital Canning distinguished between direct and indirect valuation; direct valuation was the calculation of the present value where future cash flows could be measured reliably, while indirect valuation was any other process which was adopted as a surrogate in the absence of reliability.[1] The income models which are derived from the various valuation bases might be viewed similarly – that is, economic income as the ideal measurement, with other forms as surrogates in the absence of reliable input to the economic model.

The economic income measurement looks to the future and to plans and expectations. This is in stark contrast to the historical models – both the historical cost and current value models – which are concerned with the consequences of the past. In a perfect world where there is no uncertainty there will be no actual variations from expectations and therefore no adjustments to the "ex ante" measurement of income. In the real and imperfect world, however, there will be changes, perhaps many and significant, to expectations, and unexpected or "windfall" gains and losses will arise. These changes can be caused by differences either in the amount or timing of cash flows or in the expectation of them and by changes (say) to the interest rate. Whether these gains can be properly regarded as income depends on the capital concept, and this is discussed later.

The changes for actual experience and revised expectations can be made from the end of a period in a revised ex post measurement of economic income for the past and in a revised ex ante measurement of the entity's (remaining) future. Ex post income, if measured without the precedent of an ex ante model with which to compare realities with expectations, is little more than a theoretical exercise which serves to demonstrate the approach, particularly at the end of an entity's life when all facts are known. There is no complication of revisions to expectations, and windfall gains, because there is certainty from the end vantage point. Windfall gains, however, can still arise from the difference between the computed economic value of capital at the outset and the capital actually invested. This is demonstrated in our example below.

As indicated above, periodic income has little relevance in the economic model. The emphasis is on the total expected cash flows for the entire time horizon, whenever these flows are anticipated, and it is the discounting of these to present value which is important to give a total amount for capital at a given point. This, therefore, avoids the many arbitrary recognition, matching and allocation procedures of some other models. The distinction between capital and income is de-emphasised with income being an extension of capital; that is, the flows, and the stocks they represent, are really one and the same thing, separated essentially by time. From this it can be seen that an income statement and a balance sheet in the more traditional form also have less relevance.

Four determinant factors

There are four factors in the computation of economic income. If the model is ex ante, they will be based on prediction; if ex post, they are based on fact. These factors are:

(1) the source of all cash inflows and outflows
(2) the amounts of such flows
(3) the timing of each cash flow
(4) the discount rate to be applied.

Having determined each of these factors and the classification of windfall gains, if any, the economic income can be calculated. Clearly the ex ante model is fraught with uncertainty. The amounts and timing of cash flows will range in confidence level from near certainty, as in the case of the repayment of a loan in the near future, to an inspired guess, as in the case of anticipated receipts from the marketing of a new product. Determination of the discount factor, which should embrace both a financing rate and a risk factor, can be complex and, like the cash flows, subject to much revision.

Illustration

Using the data from the Prologue the economic income model can be demonstrated. The ex post approach at the end of year 3 has been selected as the more convenient to explain (all amounts in £s):

Cash received by Mr X on close of business at end of year 3	23,500
Discount factor (1)	10% pa

	Capital value Beginning of year	End of year	Difference = Income (3)	Windfall gain
Year 1 (2)	17,656	19,421	1,765	3,856 (4)
Year 2	19,421	21,363	1,942	
Year 3	21,363	23,500	2,137	

Notes to illustration

(1) The discount rate of 10% is the firm's funding rate as charged by the bank on the loan. If the economic income were being computed ex ante at (say) the beginning of year 1, this rate probably would be higher to include the degree of risk involved; this feature is considered below at Note 5.

(2) Using year 1 as an example, the value of the opening capital is the discounted present value of £23,500 to be received in three years' time; in valuing closing capital for year 1 the receipt of £23,500 is only two years' away. Thus:

$$\text{Opening} - \frac{23{,}500}{1.10^3} = 17{,}656$$

$$\text{Closing} - \frac{23{,}500}{1.10^2} = 19{,}421$$

(These calculations are based on the discounting formula, $P_0 = a/(1 + i)n$ where P_0 is the present value of the cash flow
a is the future amount to be received
i is the discount rate
n is the number of years to wait.)

(3) The income in any year is derived by deducting the value of opening capital from closing capital; it is the equivalent of 10% of the opening economic capital.

(4) Because the ex post approach was adopted, no windfall gains arose during the three years of the firm's operating life. While, however, such gains are avoided by the ex post approach, they can still arise at the beginning of the investment – as they do in this case. The gain is computed as follows:

Discounted present value of closing capital of £23,500 at beginning of year 1	£17,656
Capital invested at beginning of year 1	13,800
Windfall gain	£3,856

This windfall might be considered merely a restatement of opening capital, or it might be thought of as income if, for example, the decision to invest in the business was perceived as a critical event. The classification of windfall gains is discussed later.

This gain is made up of gains variously classified by the other income models as a mixture of operating and holding gains. Its treatment in the economic income model as a windfall gain draws attention to the de-emphasis of the more traditional income and capital distinction.

(5) Assume, however, that in an ex ante model the projections were confirmed by the data above for ex post income except that a rate of 12% was used until the end of year 2, when the 10% rate was substituted; income would then be:

	Capital value			
	Beginning of year	End of year	Difference = income	Windfall gain
Year 1	16,727	18,734	2,007	2,927
Year 2	18,734	20,982	2,248	
Change to interest rate		21,363		381
Year 3	21,363	23,500	2,137	

The windfall on the opening capital becomes £2,927 (£16,727 − £13,800) and there is a further windfall of £381 (£21,363 − £20,982) at the end of year 2 when the rate of 10% is substituted.

The recognition and timing of windfall gains can be seen to be dependent on a number of factors, including the vantage point from which the cash flows are viewed (ex ante or ex post).

Measurement property of monetary unit

The unit of measurement used with the economic income model is the monetary unit.

Asset valuation

As indicated earlier, and in our example, the traditional presentation of income statement and balance sheet does not apply. But a balance sheet can be prepared with all assets measured on the basis of discounted present value. Cash is presented at face value. Other monetary assets and liabilities can be presented at their discounted amounts if the timing of their receipt or payment is known; unless the amounts are particularly significant or the discounts rate is high most monetary items whose realisation-to-cash date is close to the balance sheet can be expressed at face value.

Presentation of individual non-monetary assets is more difficult. Aside from having to estimate future cash flows so as to discount them, there is the problem of dividing and allocating these cash flows to individual assets. Assets such as inventories can be expressed at realisable value as a reasonable surrogate and discounted according to the time span of realisation; but other assets may have to be expressed in the groups which contribute to one cash stream or even as only one group.

Related features of asset measurement under this system are the three fundamental assumptions which are used to evaluate assets – namely, the amount of cash flows, their timing and the discount rate to be used. Each of these usually represents significant problems. In the ex ante model the degree of confidence in the amount and timing of cash flows can vary considerably across the range of a firm's activities; and the expectation can also vary day by day. The discount rate is equally, if not more, difficult to determine. This rate should not only include the opportunity cost of the funds, which is the interest rate, but also take account of the assessed confidence level of receiving the cash flows at the anticipated time. The latter is the risk factor. The longer the expected time interval the greater the uncertainty and the higher the rate. This can mean using a different discount rate for each cash flow.

Concept of capital

The concept of capital is related to future expectations in being the discounted present value of the assets. Sufficient resources must be retained to preserve the future cash flows which the present values represent. Retention is affected not only by changes in expectations of cash flows but also by changes in the discount rate (as in our example). When there is a fall in interest rates the present values increase, which results in a gain. But the assessment of the risk element in the discount rate is very subjective; it may also change, causing present values to be adjusted upwards or downwards with consequences for gains and losses. These gains and losses arise without any transaction having necessarily taken place.

Classification of windfall gains

These gains arise because actual experience is different from expectations or because expectations and/or discount rates are revised. The point at issue is whether such gains should be treated as income. If they are viewed as representing surpluses after capital has been preserved intact, they can be classified as income. However, the counter-argument is that many windfall gains arise due to revised expectations which, in effect, are no more than a restatement of opening capital to correct for earlier, and less accurate, judgment.

One example of changed expectations was covered in the above example (see note 5 to example). Another is as follows:

If Mr X had anticipated an ultimate distribution of £22,000 until the end of year 2 and had only then revised his expectation of cash flow upwards to £23,500, a windfall would arise at the end of year 2:

		Capital value at 10%			
	Cash flow anticipated	Beginning of year	End of year	Difference = income	Windfall gains
Year 1 (end)	£22,000	£16,529	£18,182	£1,653	£2,729
Year 2 (end)	23,500	18,182	21,364	3,182	
				(1,364)	1,364
				1,818	
Year 3 (end)	23,500	21,364	23,500	2,136	

It can be seen that the windfall gain at the beginning of year 1 is £2,729, arising from the difference between the economic value of capital (£16,529) and capital invested (£13,800). This gain is less than that shown in the ex post model, which used the ultimate £23,500 throughout the calculations. In year 2 there is a further windfall gain of £1,364, caused by the change in expectations of the ultimate cash flow to £23,500 from the £22,000 expected hitherto (that is, £23,500 − £22,000 = £1,500, discounted at 10% for 1 year = £1,364).

The basic question is whether this £1,364 is income or simply a restatement of opening capital to rectify an erroneous earlier expectation. If the original expectation is demonstrated to be erroneous through a change in circumstances, this may strengthen the argument for classifying the gain as income (consider a substantial change to world raw material prices, for example, oil).

If such a change is regarded as a restatement of opening capital, then it would be added at the beginning of year 1 at its then present value of £1,127 (that is, £1,500 discounted at 10% for 3 years = £1,127). This £1,127 is the difference between the value of the opening capital shown above (£16,529) and that in the earlier ex post example (£17,656). Additionally there may be changing capital needs through expansion and contraction and any such changes must first be considered before determining the amount which can be spent without impairing revised capital (changing capital needs, arising from asset replacement and distribution policies, apply to all income models).

The case for the economic income model

(1) In ex ante form the economic income measurement can play a large part in management decision-making, with its emphasis on future expectations. This is particularly so with specific project evaluations rather than when used as a comprehensive system of income measurement in the way which this Chapter has addressed it. Thus, competing investment projects can be evaluated more accurately by taking account of the time factor in projected cash flows by discounting. Additionally "hold or sell" decisions are easier to make when the economic value of an asset, or group of assets, or even entire firms, is compared with realisable value; if the latter is higher the asset(s) should be sold.
Comment Alternatively this information could also form the basis of a review of business strategy on how to bring economic value up to realisable value. The point is that the information appears to be useful.

(2) The system is already used extensively in the life assurance industry to measure profit by determining the present values of both assets and liabilities. This demonstrates that, while subjective, it has practicality.

(3) The valuation process is particularly useful when applied to monetary assets and liabilities where the amounts are known with confidence but significant time intervals have to elapse before receipt and payment. An example is lease obligations where both the asset and the liability arising are reported.

(4) The discounting process makes the values reported comparable over time.

(5) The ex ante model is timely in that it provides information before the event rather than after it; it is also highly relevant.

The case against the economic income model

(1) The information used in the ex ante model is highly subjective, such as the amount and timing of cash flows, and the interest rate and risk factor which go to make the discount rate. It could be extremely difficult for certain categories of user, such as shareholders and other groups external to the entity, to use information in any practical way with this degree of subjectivity, the more so when the assessment of the risk factor is considered with its reflection of individual preference and potential volatility.
Comment None the less for many user groups, such as management, the information can be very useful. It is also worth bearing in mind that many decisions to invest in an entity are taken partly on the basis of trading and cash flow forecasts; such data forms the raw material for economic income measurement.

(2) The expectations on which the model is based are not only highly subjective but also highly variable.

(3) The estimates produced cannot be verified.

(4) A strong reason for measuring income is to enable more accurate predictions to be made about the future, but with the ex ante model the income is actually measured from these predictions. Thus, the income relates only to the future; past operations and transactions are ignored.

(5) Income, therefore, cannot represent the quality of management decisions and performance because it is based on future expectations and predictions. Performance can only be assessed by reference to the past.

(6) The results produced are frequently changed as expectations and assessment of risk change; this creates instability in the income measurement.
Comment The degree of instability does not arise in other income models because the attempts to anticipate the various facets which comprise the economic future are not so

intensive nor extensive. This instability therefore is the price paid for focusing on the future to such a degree.

(7) Income is measured and presented as one amount without any analysis of reasons being available; for example, how much relates to operations and good management and how much is good luck?
Comment Having determined the income measurement it is then possible to analyse it into its main constituents; this analysis is simply more subjective than with other income models.

(8) The emphasis is on the time factor and cash flows. While these are undoubtedly important, other economic activities are excluded.

(9) The continuous revisions of expectations and discount rates give rise to windfall gains. These must be treated carefully if capital is not to be eroded; for example, how much of these gains is a restatement of opening capital?

(10) Many assets, especially those held for use in the longer term, cannot be measured independently because of the problem of allocating cash flows to them individually.

The economic ex ante income measurement is not proposed by supporters as an alternative comprehensive approach, even though it is sometimes described as the ideal theoretical system. The severe practical limitations alone are sufficient to question its feasibility, particularly those relating to the substantial uncertainties and subjective judgments involved in predicting the amounts and timing of cash flows and in selecting the appropriate discount rate. In the context of project analysis, however, depending on the degree of uncertainty accompanying the predictions, the approach provides information which is relevant and, taken as complementary to the historical systems (of either historical cost or current value), can be useful for decision-making.

Reference

1. J. B. Canning, *Economics of Accountancy*, Ronald Press, 1929, page 182, referred to by E. S. Hendriksen in *Accounting Theory* (3rd edition), Richard D. Irwin Inc, 1977, page 264.

8 The Mixed Value to the Firm Income Model

Brief history

The current and future value systems discussed in the preceding three chapters identified a single valuation concept in each case. With the current value approaches it is either the cost to replace resources (the buying or entry price) or the realisable value of the resources (the selling or exit price); the future value basis is the economic value which relies on the discounted present value of anticipated future cash flows. In contrast, the value to the firm basis is a comprehensive and formal adoption of a mixed value approach which in defined circumstances can utilise one of these three concepts. Thus, the valuation of a firm's capital can be made up of a mixed bag of bases.

The value to the firm basis is taken from the work in 1937 of Bonbright, who applied the principle in considering compensation for the loss of property:

> The value of a property to its owner is identical in amount with the adverse value of the entire loss, direct and indirect, that the owner might expect to suffer if he were to be deprived of the property.[1]

In the mid-1960s to mid-1970s various writers developed the idea further for accounting purposes. Then in 1975, in the UK, the Government-sponsored Sandilands Committee produced a 364-page report recommending adoption of the same principle:

> Assets should be shown at their "value to the business". In the majority of cases this will be their written down current replacement cost (or current purchase price) but may in some cases be their net realisable value or "economic value".[2]

Following this recommendation, which the Sandilands Committee called "current cost accounting", the professional accounting bodies in the UK, through a series of exposure drafts and guidelines, eventually published SSAP No 16 in 1980.[3] This applied the flesh to the skeleton of the Sandilands Report and added some further ideas to the original. SSAP 16 was issued partly as an experiment and exempted certain defined smaller entities. Not all its features met with approval, however, and, in turn, proposals for its modification were made in 1984 in Exposure Draft 35, more generically entitled "Accounting for the Effects of Changing Prices".[4]

What is value to the firm?

Value to the firm can be stated as the deprival, or opportunity, value – that is, the lowest cost avoided by the act of owning the asset. This is the opposite of the opportunity cost (or current cash equivalent) concept which represents the most profitable alternative which is foregone in taking the proposed route.

The assets of a firm can be held for further use or sold; if they are sold they can either be replaced or not. This gives the three bases of valuation: if an asset is held for further use the potentially relevant basis is economic value ("EV"); if intent on sale it is realisable value ("RV")[5]; and if it will be replaced, the appropriate basis is replacement cost ("RC"). The deprival value is established for each asset, or group of assets, by identifying the most appropriate action in each case and adopting the valuation base accordingly. Since there are three options open, there are six permutations of relative values:

	Basis selected	
(1) RC > RV > EV	RV	See discussion below
(2) RC > EV > RV	EV	
(3) RV > RC > EV	RC	
(4) RV > EV > RC	RC	
(5) EV > RC > RV	RC	
(6) EV > RV > RC	RC	

In case (1) realisable value is greater than economic value but less than replacement cost. The asset would be sold because proceeds of sale are greater than the present value of anticipated proceeds through holding the asset for further use. And, since the cost to replace is higher than proceeds from immediate sale or extended "sale" through further use, it would not be replaced. The most relevant value of this asset, therefore, is realisable value.

In case (2) economic value through continued use is greater than the proceeds of immediate sale, so the asset would not be sold; neither would it be replaced, because the cost of doing this is greater than the proceeds expected through use. Economic value, then, is the most appropriate basis.

Case (3) shows that immediate sale is more attractive than holding for continued use. But since the replacement cost is lower, the asset would be replaced and immediately sold time and again until market supply and demand conditions changed the buying/selling price relationship. By owning the asset the lowest cost avoided is the buying price or replacement cost and this would be the valuation basis here.

With case (4) immediate sale is again more attractive than continued use, but this time the cost to replace is lower than both. Again, therefore, the asset would be replaced repeatedly, making the replacement cost the most relevant basis.

Case (5) indicates that continued use is more attractive than immediate sale. However, the replacement cost is lower and represents the lowest cost avoided by owning the asset.

Case (6) also shows that continued use is more attractive than immediate sale. Again, however, cost to replace is lower, this time, than both exit values. Replacement cost, therefore, is the appropriate basis.

The backing given to the concept of value to the firm by the professional accounting bodies in the UK may suggest a general acceptance which, in fact, is spurious. There are many and learned discussions and criticisms of it, coverage of which is outside the scope of this text. Suffice it to say that some propose amendments, others outright rejection of the concept. None the less deprival value is being adopted in practice and has many supporters.

The measurement of income which is produced from the value to the firm concept is similar to that obtained from using the replacement cost system. Given the capital concept of operating capacity, income is derived by matching against revenues the value of assets consumed in generating those revenues. These expenses of consumption are either replacement costs or expenses derived from the evaluation of assets on a realisable value or economic value basis; they are sometimes known collectively as the "current costs". It can be seen that, as with the replacement cost system, the usual trigger point for operating income determination is the deemed realisation and recognition of revenue.

Illustration

Using the data given at the Prologue the value to the firm approach can be demonstrated. In doing so the version promulgated by ED 35 has been adopted, including the features peculiar to it and its forerunner SSAP 16. The historical cost information reported in Chapter 3 has been used as the starting point (all amounts in £s):

	Year 1	Year 2	Year 3 (before close)	Year 3 (after close)	Total
INCOME STATEMENT					
Historical cost reported income	400	2,400	3,400	3,500	
Current cost adjustments					
– for depreciation (1) (2)	(400)	(1,000)	(1,400)		
– for gain on sale of property (3)				(3,500)	
– gearing (4)	13	—	—		
	(387)	(1,000)	(1,400)	(3,500)	
Current cost income due to proprietor (5)	13	1,400	2,000	—	3,413
BALANCE SHEET (6)					
Property – at replacement cost (7)	8,900	9,900	11,500	—	
Vans – at net replacement cost (7)	6,000	3,600	—	—	
	14,900	13,500	11,500	—	
Cash	3,000	8,000	14,000	23,500	
Total assets	17,900	21,500	25,500	23,500	
representing –					
Capital – opening	13,800	13,800	13,800	13,800	
Holding gains					
– property (7)	900	1,900	3,500	3,500	
– vans (7)	1,200	3,000	4,200	4,200	
backlog depn (8)	—	(600)	(1,400)	(1,400)	
	1,200	2,400	2,800	2,800	
	15,900	18,100	20,100	20,100	
Gearing adjustment (4)	(13)	(13)	(13)	(13)	
Income	13	1,413	3,413	3,413	
	15,900	19,500	23,500	23,500	
Bank loan	2,000	2,000	2,000	—	
	17,900	21,500	25,500	23,500	

Notes to illustration

(1) This represents the difference between depreciation charged on a historical cost basis and a current cost basis; in this case the latter is the same as replacement cost depreciation:

	Year 1	2	3
Historical cost (Chapter 3)	£2,600	£2,600	£2,600
Replacement cost (Chapter 5)	3,000	3,600	4,000
Additional charge	£(400)	£(1,000)	£(1,400)

(2) The adoption of replacement cost in note 1 as the current cost (or value to the firm) follows the comparison of the three valuation bases as follows:

	Year 1	2	3
Property – EV		see below	
– RC	£8,900	£9,900	£11,500
– RV	8,800	9,700	11,500
Vans – EV		see below	
– RC	6,000	3,600	—
– RV	5,800	3,000	—

The firm is profitable and the economic value of the property and vans is assumed to be higher than realisable values; therefore the firm would continue to use them. This means that cost to replace represents the lowest cost avoided by ownership.

(3) (a) The historical cost gain on sale of property of £3,500 has to be adjusted so as to compare proceeds with the costs to replace at the time of sale. The unrealised holding gains representing the price changes to property have been recorded in the balance sheet at each accounting date (as they were in the replacement cost model):

Proceeds of sale	£11,500
Replacement cost	11,500
Current cost gain	—
Historical cost gain	3,500
Adjustment	(£3,500)

The historical cost gain has been reflected in the value to the firm model as holding gains thus:

Year 1	£900
Year 2	1,000
Year 3	1,600
	£3,500

(b) A further adjustment, the monetary working capital adjustment, is required by the ED 35 version of value to the firm accounting (originating in SSAP 16); this is shown below for illustration but has not been reflected in the example. It is designed to charge operating profit with the change to prices which has occurred during the time-lag when monetary working capital was held. While its computation may look similar to an adjustment for loss of purchasing power it is, quite specifically, not related to that. Cash may form part of working capital depending on the facts. In our example it is clear that cash is not, in fact, working capital; instead it is being accumulated for eventual distribution to Mr X. If it were working capital the computation of the adjustment would be as follows:

	Year 1	Year 2	Year 3
Opening balance	£ —	£3,000	£8,000
Closing balance	3,000	8,000	14,000
Average, assuming an even build-up	1,500	5,500	11,000
	×	×	×
Relevant prices movement (usually related to purchases and sales prices but here assumed to be the same as the general index)	$\frac{110 - 100}{100}$	$\frac{121 - 110}{110}$	$\frac{132 - 121}{121}$
=	£(150)	£(550)	£(1,000)

(4) The gearing adjustment is another feature of the ED 35 version of value to the firm accounting which was not proposed by the Sandilands Committee. ED 35, in fact, makes three methods of computing a gearing adjustment available. This reflects the considerable controversy and debate which have arisen about this adjustment. The three methods available are:

(a) Abate the realised holding gains, which form the adjustments to the historical cost income statement, *and* the unrealised holding gains, in the form of current cost revaluation surpluses (and deficits), by the proportion of these gains which are financed by outside creditors but which accrue to the shareholders. This method was originally proposed for current cost accounting in the late 1970s.

(b) Abate only the realised holding gains by the proportion explained at paragraph (a). This method, originating in the requirements of SSAP 16, is the one followed in our example.

(c) Calculate the effect of general price changes on the net borrowing by applying the change in a general price index to the average net borrowing for the period. This method is quite different from the other two. It aims to show, when combined with interest charges (or receipts), the net interest charge in "real terms".[6]

After this adjustment the derived amount represents the current cost profit. The calculation, using the method at paragraph (b), is as follows:

	Year 1	2	3
Adjustments to historical cost income	£400	£1,000	£1,400
Current cost of operating assets (assumed to accrue evenly)		N/A	
– Property (£8,000 + £8,900) ÷ 2 =	8,450	see below	
– Vans (£7,800 + £6,000) ÷ 2 =	6,500		
Net operating assets	15,350		
Net borrowing – bank loan	2,000	2,000	2,000
less: average balance of surplus cash (see Note 3(b))	(1,500)	(5,500)	(11,000)
Net borrowing	500	N/A	N/A
Gearing (borrowing : operating assets)	50:15,350	N/A	N/A
as percentage	= 3.26%		
Adjustment 3.26% × £400	= £13		

Clearly the £13 is not material and in practice would probably not be adjusted for. It has been processed here for illustration. It is charged against capital. The principle is similar to that discussed in Chapter 5 in considering monetary liabilities, the essential difference between the two calculations being that the effect of the Chapter 5 approach is to include realised and unrealised holding gains (that is, the method covered at paragraph (a) above) while our version applies only to realized gains. The cash surplus to operating requirements has to be deducted from external finance in computing our gearing adjustment. In years 2 and 3 this resulted in an excess of surplus cash, thereby eliminating the need for this adjustment.

(5) It can be seen that the current cost income is not determined until all current cost adjustments are processed against the historical cost income model. An alternative presentation, permitted by ED 35 and originating in SSAP 16, is firstly to determine the operating profit by deducting the current cost adjustments for depreciation and working capital from the historical cost profit (before interest). This operating profit represents the income from operations; that is, it excludes any unrealised holding gains. Secondly, the subsequent adjustment for gearing is matched with the interest costs and the net amount is then deducted from operating profit to give current cost income; that is, income earned by the shareholders of the entity as opposed to the entity itself.

(6) A balance sheet is not required by ED 35 (although it was by the earlier SSAP 16); instead selective information on current costs of fixed assets and inventories is required in note form.

(7) As indicated at note 2, property and vans are stated at replacement cost. Holding gains arising are included as part of capital.

(8) Backlog depreciation arises because of the use of replacement costs. The discussion and the detail of the calculations are given in Chapter 5.

Measurement property of monetary unit

It can be seen that the value to the firm system adopts the monetary unit as the unit of measurement in common with the three valuation approaches on which it is based. This means that all price changes are based on specific prices. However, as indicated in Chapter 5 when discussing the replacement cost model, the effect of general inflation could be calculated and identified separately and the remainder deemed to represent the relative (or "real") movement on asset prices.

Asset valuation

As already discussed, asset valuation is the lowest cost avoided by ownership of the asset or the amount of loss suffered if deprived of it and is a choice from whichever of the three bases of replacement cost, realisable value and economic value represents deprival value. It was mentioned when discussing replacement cost accounting that there was not necessarily any specific intention to invest in replacement and that this is an investment decision rather than an accounting one. The same applies to the value to the firm basis. Selection of the valuation basis does not necessarily imply that assets will be replaced, sold or retained in use; asset replacement policy is a separate issue.

Concept of capital

Capital is represented by the value to the firm of its assets. This attempts to "tune" the capital valuation more specifically to the most economically logical use to which the assets should be put (although, as mentioned above, it does not imply intention by management). By doing so, it is argued, the valuation of capital and charges for its maintenance should make the information more realistic, more relevant and, therefore, more useful to users. A criticism of each of the three valuation bases from which the value to the firm is selected is that they are too restrictive and inflexible in isolation; and that the very exercise of choice available from the three bases demonstrates this.

The concept is not related per se to the physical assets of the firm but to its operating capacity (or capability). Operating capacity can mean several different things. For example, it can have an exclusively physical context and mean the physical assets of property, plant and equipment and inventories; this was the concept advocated by the Sandilands Report.[7] Again operating capacity might relate to the volume of goods and services which a firm can supply, and might include not only physical assets but also monetary working capital. This approach was favoured by SSAP 16[8] with the refinement that the capacity so measured should be abated by the proportion which was funded by long-term, non-proprietorial liabilities; and is continued by ED 35[9] with the additional refinement of the choice of three methods for calculating the gearing adjustment. There are further questions about whether monetary working capital should properly include all cash, or some of it, and whether current liabilities should be deducted as required by the ED 35 version (and its SSAP 16 predecessor).

In each case the value to the firm of the relevant assets is determined and a maintenance charge against periodic income is made for the value consumed in the process of earning income. Again, however, the problem of backlog depreciation may arise as it did in the replacement cost model. To the extent that this depreciation is not charged against income the latter may be overstated and operating capacity may not be preserved if this income is distributed; distribution policy, however, is an issue separate from income measurement. Backlog depreciation has already been discussed in Chapter 5, where it was said that, so long as depreciation provisions charged against income were invested immediately in new equipment, in general the problem can be more apparent than real.

As indicated when discussing the current cash equivalent model in Chapter 6, it is possible to introduce a charge against income representing a provision for the maintenance of financial capital on (say) a general purchasing power basis. This basis is quite separate, and different, from that followed for asset valuation.

Working capital can be divided between inventories and monetary working capital. The usual rule is applied to inventories in choosing the basis (although economic value in use is not usually relevant here). Monetary working capital, when included in operating capacity, can comprise such items as debtors and trade creditors and possibly bank overdraft and cash if these are considered part of operating capital. Each amount, being monetary, is valued at face value. The maintenance charge against income for monetary working capital is peculiar to ED 35 (and its predecessor SSAP 16), although variations of it have now appeared in the professional promulgations of other countries. This charge was illustrated in the notes to our example above. The charge is intended to eliminate the effect of specific price changes which can occur while monetary working capital is held.

Classification of holding gains

In emphasising the operating capacity of the firm, holding gains are regarded not as income but, in effect, as a restatement of capital caused by price changes. All such gains are banished from the income measurement, which leaves the latter as an operating income (with the gearing adjustment made subsequently in the ED 35 version). This is not to ignore holding gains. As indicated earlier in the discussion of the replacement cost model (Chapter 5), these gains can be regarded as cost savings and can be of greater significance to the user than operating income in some circumstances.

The case for the value to the firm income model

The system is based on the current value and future value models, all of which have merits in their own right, and it is not intended to reiterate them here. The value to the firm approach exploits the most appropriate features of these models, in given circumstances, and the claim is made that this flexibility of choice makes the information particularly relevant and useful. It has also been demonstrated by UK experience to be practical to implement.
Comment The same UK experience has also demonstrated significant opposition to the approach. For example, the professional accounting bodies in the UK published the report of the CCA Monitoring Working Party in 1983, which indicated that there was a need to alter SSAP 16 substantially and that, among other things, different methods of calculating the effects of changing prices should be permitted; the same report also indicated a need to simplify SSAP 16[10 11]. The subsequently published ED 35[12] has done little to respond to the fundamental criticisms of SSAP 16, the changes being primarily concerned with scope of application, presentation and a choice of gearing adjustment.

The case against the value to the firm income model

The three valuation systems which are used all have disadvantages which were identified earlier and will not be repeated here (see Chapters 5, 6 and 7). However, the value to the firm concept runs into additional criticism peculiar to it:

(1) The validity of the choice in the valuation mechanism (RC v RV v EV) is seriously challenged. In particular the elimination of economic value and realisable values in four out of the six permutations is challenged as inappropriate for investor use. On a similar theme its use as a basis of income measurement is seen by some as irrelevant, the only attraction being the usefulness in the valuation of assets. Further criticism is based on the volatility of values which change as business confidence about the future varies; yet such confidence is the input to the income measurement.

(2) The basis is "what if" accounting. The assets are already held and the continued holding, sale or replacement decisions are hypothetical because they have yet to be made. The continued use of the assets justifies the economic value basis (or a surrogate in the face of economic value impracticalities). Again, the question "what if the firm were deprived of the asset?" is hypothetical because it has not been deprived. It is misleading to measure income on the basis of such hypotheses.
Comment Eventually, through use, the firm will be deprived of the asset (though not necessarily the resources it represents). The question "what if" then becomes relevant.

(3) By mixing the values available for selection as value to the firm the result is a heterogeneous non-additive list of values and a measurement of income which is meaningless or, at least, difficult to interpret. Such difficulty seriously impairs any usefulness.
Comment The values are heterogeneous at base level, but when considered at the higher level of the value to the firm more homogeneity is suggested.

Despite these serious criticisms the value to the firm concept is in active use in the UK and has been demonstrated to be practicable; there appears to be, however, a continuing lack of consensus and the UK approach may well be modified eventually. The degree to which the income measurement can be interpreted accurately in any given case may depend upon how extensively the replacement cost basis is selected in practice as the value in use or upon how close are the values on all three bases. While the replacement cost basis also has its critics, the information produced is more easily understood. In contrast the subtlety of the value to the firm concept may not be fully realised.

References and notes

1. J. C. Bonbright, *The Valuation of Property*, McGraw-Hill, 1937, page 71.
2. F. E. P. Sandilands, "Inflation Accounting", Report of the Inflation Accounting Committee, HMSO, 1975, page 56.
3. "Current Cost Accounting", Statement of Standard Accounting Practice No 16, Accounting Standards Committee, 1980. The process of development of SSAP No 16 could be described as tortuous. Following the publication of the Sandilands Report (qv), Provisional Statement of Standard Accounting Practice No 7, which had recommended an indexed based purchasing power approach to inflation accounting, was withdrawn. Exposure Draft No 18, "Current Cost Accounting" was published in 1976 but was withdrawn in 1977 following strong opposition to it. This was followed by "Inflation Accounting – An Interim Recommendation", published in 1977 which was superseded by the publication of the Exposure Draft which led to SSAP 16 being issued.
4. "Accounting for the Effects of Changing Prices", Exposure Draft 35, Accounting Standards Committee, 1984.
5. SSAP 16 and ED 35 refer to economic value and net realisable value collectively as "recoverable amount".
6. ED 35, paragraph 20.
7. F. E. P. Sandilands, "Inflation Accounting", Report of the Inflation Accounting Committee, see, for example, page 163.
8. "Current Cost Accounting", SSAP 16.
9. "Accounting for the Effects of Changing Prices", ED 35.
10. "Interim Report of the CCA Monitoring Working Party", Accounting Standards Committee, April 1983; followed by "Report of the CCA Monitoring Working Party", Accounting Standards Committee, September 1983.
11. There were other sources of confirmed opposition to SSAP 16, as originally issued, including a resolution against its compulsory application to all entities in July 1982 to the members of The Institute of Chartered Accountants in England and Wales; this was only rejected by a narrow majority.
12. "Accounting for the Effects of Changing Prices", ED 35.

9 Summary; Other Measures of Economic Activity

Summary of results

This text has considered six of the main theories of income measurement, including a method of applying price-level restatement, each of which, for illustration purposes, was applied to historical cost data. Using the same common data provided in the Prologue, income was measured according to the philosophy of each system. These measurements reported the following (all amounts in £s except for purchasing power method, which is in £ppu's):

Income concept	Income in year 1	2	3	Holding gains (or windfalls)	Total
Historical cost	400	2,400	3,400	3,500	9,700
General purchasing power applied to historical cost	340	1,754	2,023	940	5,057
Replacement cost	—	1,400	2,000	6,300	9,700
Current cash equivalent (before capital maintenance adjustment)	1,800	3,100	4,800	—	9,700
Economic value (ex post)	1,765	1.942	2,137	3,856	9,700
Value to the firm	13	1,400	2,000	6,287	9,700

It is interesting to note that the holding gains arising under the replacement cost and value to the firm models become income only at the point when Mr X decides to close down the business. At that point he has changed his capital concept to a personal one quite unrelated to that which he would follow if he decided to continue in business. This continuity, so stressed by the replacement cost concept, does not apply in the same context to the current cash equivalent model, which is why all the £9,700 is anticipated as income under that system.

Note also that the £5,060 reported by the current cash equivalent model, after inflation adjustment (see Chapter 6), represents a difference of £4,640 from the £9,700 of income and holding gains reported by all the other models which did not take account of general price inflation. This difference is the aggregate of the charges for the maintenance of the purchasing power of capital – namely £1,380 in year 1, £1,560 in year 2 and £1,700 in year 3.

Summary of key variables

The problem of income measurement is directly related to the demand for periodic appraisal and the attention which this focuses on incomplete transactions. These incomplete transactions are assessed by a variety of means and it is this variety which causes the same periodic economic activity to be reported with such disparate results. In essence, there are four key variables, which were identified in Chapter 1 as:

(1) the measurement property of the monetary unit
(2) the asset valuation basis
(3) the concept of capital
(4) the classification of holding gains.

These variables can be presented in tabular form for each of the systems which have been reviewed:

SUMMARY

Income model	Measurement property of monetary unit	Asset valuation	Concept of capital to be maintained	Classification of holding gains (or windfalls)
Historical cost	Medium of exchange	Original (historical) cost	Initial money investment by shareholders	Income when realised
General purchasing power	Purchasing power	Original valuation basis, restated in units of purchasing power	Purchasing power of initial money investment	Do not arise; inflationary movements go to restate capital
Replacement cost	Medium of exchange	Current cost to replace	Productive capacity of assets either in physical or money terms	If capital is operating capital, capital; if capital is money value, income
Current cash equivalent	Medium of exchange	Current realisable value of exchangeable assets in orderly disposal	Purchasing power of shareholders' interest	Income
Economic income	Medium of exchange	Discounted present value of future cash flows	Discounted present value of assets	Income or capital
Value to the firm	Medium of exchange	Deprival value chosen from most appropriate of replacement cost, realisable value and economic value	Value to the firm of the operating capacity	Capital

Periodic income; an elusive and fragile concept

These key variables serve to underline how critical is the timing of the recognition of economic activity in the periodic measurement of income; for example, when revenue is recognised, when expenses are recognised and allocated and when price changes are recognised. There is also the importance with which some view the classification of gains between operating, holding and inflationary gains, although others would regard the operating/holding analysis as arbitrary. In the long term, whether gains are made because of the production of goods and services (operating gains) or the holding of goods while prices are rising (holding gains) is of less relevance. However, the effect of inflation continues to matter because of its effect on the general purchasing power of the ultimate sums distributed to the proprietors.

The same importance applies to the other contentious issues which each system produces – for example, the realisation concept and cost allocation procedures of historical cost accounting, the determination of monetary gains and losses using purchasing power accounting, the treatment of backlog depreciation under the replacement cost system, the going concern interpretation of the current cash equivalent measurement, the determination of the discount rate in the economic income model and the validity of the choice of valuation bases available under the value to the firm approach. Upon how each of these issues, and others, is resolved in any particular case will depend the amount described as the income for the period.

The effect of the four key variables, compounded by the impact of all the other factors touched on above, indicates what an elusive and fragile concept periodic income is. Clearly, however, no single concept is more relevant and more useful for all potential users; the choice of the most suitable depends on the purpose for which it is intended.

Conditions for unique measurement of income

To demonstrate how unrealistic it is to search for the "holy grail" of the one single most suitable concept of measuring periodic income in all circumstances Barton identified the three conditions which must prevail to achieve this unique, one and only, measurement:

(1) Cost and market values must remain equal through time. There would be no price changes and there would be perfect competition to ensure that no "pure" (that is non production) profits arose. There would be, therefore, only one rate of return and one discount rate. This would mean that there would be an unchanging periodic income. Historically based measures of

assets (and, therefore, capital) would give the same outcome as that indicated by economic value.

(2) The unit of measurement must be stable, meaning that all expressions in the money terms would be homogeneous.

(3) There must be certainty. Only if the future is known with certainty can increases in net wealth be allocated accurately to periods. Since certainty implies no financial risk, there would be no loss or reward for taking risks.

He goes on to indicate the consequences of any of these conditions not being met. Divergence of cost and market values means that several differing measurements of assets, capital and hence periodic income can be made. Lack of stability in the measuring unit precludes aggregation of units of different vintages. Less than complete certainty means assumptions about the future, estimates and risk taking. Differing assumptions will be made about the same future.[1]

While it might be inferred that the main concepts of income are competing, they have aspects which are really complementary. For example, the historically based systems look backwards to the past, in part as a report on stewardship, either in historical cost or current value terms, and in part as a basis for decisions about the future. The future value system looks forward as a guide to making decisions, but to do so has to make projections based in part on past experience. As another illustration, the replacement cost system is based on the continuity of operations and, therefore, is rightly concerned about provisions for the replacement of the capacity which helps to perpetuate these operations; it is concerned with the medium to long term. In contrast the current cash equivalent system emphasises the adaptability of firms in the short term.

These systems are not necessarily competing. For one purpose and user, continuity and the long term may be important; for another, adaptability and the short term may have priority. The historical cost system has run into substantial, sometimes vociferous, criticism and demands for its replacement by another approach which recognises specific price changes and general price changes, or both, as these occur. Yet for all that such replacement implies competition, the historical cost base would probably be required as the starting point for another more sophisticated and sensitive system. So again there are features which are complementary. The text has also covered the adoption of a capital concept which is on a basis quite different from that used in valuing assets, so further extending the complementary nature of the different systems.

In short, users may need income measured on more than one basis for some purposes or on different bases at different times for different purposes; because of this diversity the needs of the whole population of users are not universally the same at any one time.

In reporting to shareholders, for example, there are, at one end of the spectrum of reasonable possibilities, annual financial statements, which are prepared, usually on an historical cost basis, and used by a wide variety of varyingly informed users for a wide variety of purposes to varying degrees of satisfaction. At the other end of this information spectrum there are financial statements, prepared (say) quarterly and on at least several bases of asset valuation and capital concept – the "multi-column" approach; yet this approach encounters criticism because it is perceived by some that it is an admission by the preparers (and auditors) that they have neither the knowledge nor the expertise to decide which is the most appropriate information and to restrict presentation to that information only. And this is despite the fact, patently obvious in the development of much financial information used internally by an entity's management, that a prerequisite to the determination of what is the "most appropriate" information is a knowledge of the use and purposes intended. Whichever approach is adopted it will not satisfy all users. Conversely there seems little doubt that a fruitful direction for further research would be into the various needs and wants of the many users of this kind of financial information.

Given the wide range of interpretations available of the same economic events and activity, the question which must now be asked is "why bother?". Even allowing for the lack of a single "best" concept and the complementary advantages of the income models available, the flexibility and fragility of the information provided has brought into question the relevance and usefulness of the periodic income measurement.

Cash flow statements

There are signs that the past pre-eminence of income measurement may be less emphatic in the future as other measurements of economic activity are developed. Of these the most popular appears to be the cash flow statement. Precisely what is included as cash or near-cash will vary, depending on the purpose of the statement and the circumstances. Cash may be narrowly defined as just that – cash and other currency balances. Alternatively it may be thought of in a wider context to include all monetary assets and liabilities. Supporters of the cash flow statement regard the information it provides as particularly relevant and claim three especial advantages over the income measurement. Firstly, it emphasises the critical fact that profit earned is not necessarily manifested in cash at the time of being earned; that is, profit and liquidity are not necessarily the same thing. Secondly, it gives useful information on the ability of the firm to survive. No matter how profitable an enterprise is, its incomplete transactions, manifested for example in inventories and debtors, have to be funded as do any intended distributions to proprietors; and, if this funding is not achieved, there will not be any future profit. Thirdly, measurement of cash flows need not be subject to the same conceptual and judgmental issues which so plague income measurement (although the very avoidance of these issues can result in an incomplete measurement).

It will be clear that the cash flow statement is not to be confused with the funds statement (known in the UK as a statement of source and application of funds) which is usually the link between the amounts appearing in the balance sheet and the income statement and is thus dependent on the same conceptual and judgmental issues as the latter statements.[2] In contrast, the cash flow statement concentrates on cash or near-cash items and avoids the need to take account of the recognition and allocation judgments of income measurement. So it is easier to prepare the information and understand it. Thus, it is argued, income is an elusive, abstract concept while cash represents reality.

Cash flow reporting is made even more useful if its components are divided between the results of operating and other activities. There appears to be no strong opposition to the use of cash flow statements. Rather the concern is about their priority vis-à-vis the income measurement.

Value added statement

Another measure of economic activity which is attracting more attention is the statement of value added. This emphasises that an entity is engaged in many types of activity of which earning income is only one. Value added is the wealth created by an enterprise by its own and its employees' efforts which, therefore, embrace management, capital and labour. Thus, sales revenue, less materials and services bought in, represents value added, of which a part, but only a part, represents income. The remainder represents, for example, wages to employees, interest to lenders and depreciation for maintenance of equipment. This statement is not intended as a substitute for the income measurement but rather as a complement. Its basis is identical to that adopted for income measurement.[3]

Ratios for trend analysis

A third way of reporting activity, which has special relevance in presenting trends during periods of significant price changes, is the use of ratios, although the data being related in a ratio must be homogeneous. There is little point, for example, in computing a ratio based in part in 1974 £s and in part in 1983 £s. However, a trend of ratios, which is based exclusively on the £s of each year presented, neatly overcomes many of the problems associated with changing price levels. Clearly the usefulness of ratios depends on the validity of the underlying data. If, for example, the revenue recognition principles or cost allocation procedures are regarded as suspect, the ratios are likewise questionable.[4].

Effective communication and response to change

These are some examples of ways in which the economic activity of a firm and the events which affect it can be reported. They are complementary to the measurement of income, that flexible and fragile concept. In the final analysis they are all means to the end of providing information to potential users which is relevant, realistic and therefore useful. The essence of all reporting is effective communication. In the case of financial reporting it is effective communication of economic activity.

In time, with the continued development of ever more sophisticated computer technology, it may be that accounting will become part of a more co-ordinated, cohesive information industry, if it has not already become so. The only forecast that can be made with any certainty is that accounting, being dynamic, will not stand still. It is about measuring and reporting economic activity and it is therefore concerned with the activities of people. Because these activities are ever-changing, accounting will change in response and, with it, that part of accounting which is devoted to the measurement of income.

References and notes

1. A. D. Barton, *The Anatomy of Accounting*, University of Queensland Press, 1977, page 329.
2. For a fuller discussion of funds statements, see T. A. Lee, *The Funds Statement*, published for The Institute of Chartered Accountants of Scotland, The Accountants' Publishing Co. Ltd, 1974.
3. For a fuller discussion of value added statements, see M. F. Morley, *The Value Added Statement, a review of its use in Corporate Reports*, published for The Institute of Chartered Accountants of Scotland by Gee/Van Nostrand Reinhold (UK), 1978.
4. For a fuller discussion of ratio analysis, see M. F. Morley, *Ratio Analysis*, a monograph of The Institute of Chartered Accountants of Scotland, Van Nostrand Reinhold (UK), 1984.